Osprey Modelling • I

Modelling th
Harrier I and II

Glenn Ashley

Consultant editor Robert Oehler
Series editors Marcus Cowper and Nikolai Bogdanovic

First published in Great Britain in 2003 by Osprey Publishing, Elms Court, Chapel Way, Botley, Oxford OX2 9LP, United Kingdom.
Email: info@ospreypublishing.com

ISBN 1 84176 647 X

Editorial by Ilios Publishing, Oxford, UK (www.iliospublishing.com)
Design: Servis Filmsetting Ltd, Manchester, UK
Proofreading: Richard Windrow
Index by Bob Munro
Originated by Global Graphics, Czech Republic
Printed and bound by L-Rex Printing Company Ltd

03 04 05 06 07   10 9 8 7 6 5 4 3 2 1

A CIP catalogue record for this book is available from the British Library.

FOR A CATALOGUE OF ALL BOOKS PUBLISHED BY OSPREY MODELLING, MILITARY AND AVIATION PLEASE CONTACT:

Osprey Direct UK, P.O. Box 140, Wellingborough,
Northants, NN8 2FA, UK
E-mail: info@ospreydirect.co.uk

Osprey Direct USA, c/o MBI Publishing, P.O. Box 1,
729 Prospect Ave, Osceola, WI 54020, USA
E-mail: info@ospreydirectusa.com

www.ospreypublishing.com

Acknowledgments

I would like to thank a number of people and companies for their kind assistance in the production of this book. I hope sincerely I have not missed anyone but if so, I apologise in advance: Trevor Snowden (Humbrol Ltd & Airfix), Bob Sanchez (Two Bobs Decals), William Packard and Martin Brundell (Heritage Aviation). Without the great co-operation from these friends this book would not have got off the ground. A big thanks to Nikolai Bogdanovic for his support and assistance throughout.

Special thanks are due to Geoff Coughlin, Tony O'Toole, Piero de Santis, Neil Robinson and Robert Oehler for their much appreciated help on this project.

The photographic credits refer to the following sources:

GC	Geoff Coughlin
TO	Tony O'Toole
PDS	Piero de Santis
GA	Glenn Ashley

Contents

Introduction

The Harrier, long-time servant to the British and American forces as well as several smaller air arms around the world. Having been around for over 40 years now the Harrier is a familiar sight at air shows; and for nearly as long kits of the Harrier and its predecessor, the P.1127, have been on the shelves of model shops.

Indeed the father of all Harrier kits is the old Airfix 1/72-scale P.1127, first released in 1962, and later to become a collector's item until it was re-issued in the late 1990s. At the time Airfix was probably the company at the forefront of plastic modelling, releasing new kits on a regular basis. The company, along with Frog, were dedicated manufacturers of British aircraft types and during the bulk of the remaining decade the P.1127 was the only available kit of this pioneering British design.

When the aircraft entered service with the RAF in 1969, Airfix again were there to release a 1/72-scale kit of the Harrier GR.1 shortly after its service introduction. No mere update of an old kit, this was new and as different from the previous kits as the full-sized aircraft was.

Following on behind Airfix came Frog, who also released a kit of the GR.1. It seems some joint work was done as, at the time, Frog had contacts with the blossoming manufacturer from Japan, Hasegawa. A number of each company's kits and ideas were jointly marketed under each brand name. So when Frog released their GR.1 kit, it was not too long after that a GR.1 joined the ranks of the Hasegawa brand. And this was generally how things stood for a while.

1976 saw the release of possibly the most impressive kit so far, the Airfix 1/24-scale GR.1 which overtook the previously released (and now collector's item) Revell 1/32-scale kit. Both were seen as 'state of the art' at the time of their release.

The original box art from 1976 of the Hawker Harrier GR.1 from Airfix in 1/24-scale. (TO)

AIRFIX HAWKER HARRIER 24 SCALE th SUPER KIT NEW

The world's most advanced vertical take-off aircraft. Now flying with the RAF and the US Marine Corps. Capable of carrying over a two ton war load. Powered by a Rolls-Royce Pegasus engine.

SEA HARRIER FRS MK 1

ESCI

MADE IN ITALY

For several years the only significant change made was when the RAF updated its aircraft to GR.3 standard, and Airfix followed suit by doing the same to the kit. The only new kit was the Tamiya GR.1 in 1/48 scale.

As the 1980s dawned, the Harrier was thrust into the public spotlight as Britain went to war with Argentina. Just by chance around the time of the Falklands War Matchbox released a 1/72-scale Sea Harrier FRS.1 which albeit accurate in shape was very simple in terms of detail. After the war it seemed everyone wanted to build Harriers. Airfix released 1/48-scale GR.3 and FRS.1 kits as a result.

Throughout this decade newer versions of the Harrier began to be introduced into both full-size service and the modelling market. As the AV-8B and Harrier GR.5/7 were produced, so kits from Airfix and Hasegawa followed and the older moulds sold by Frog returned in various guises from Eastern Europe. For a while the full-size aircraft and the models developed seemingly in tandem.

Recently, as the tooling costs for new kits have spiralled, Airfix has recently upgraded the 1/24-scale kit into both GR.3 and FRS.1 variants and Hasegawa kits have now been reboxed by other companies such as Revell. Along with this, a blossoming sideline has been the release of resin kits and conversions for the missing variants such as the Kestrel, Harrier Trainer and indeed undeveloped project variants of the aircraft. So it does seem likely that the Harrier will form a part of the modelling scene for some time to come.

The 1/72-scale ESCI Sea Harrier FRS.1, which at the time of writing was about to be re-released under the Italeri brand. (TO)

The 1/48-scale Monogram McDonnell Douglas AV 8B Harrier, that dates from the 1980s. (TO)

MONOGRAM

SKILL 2

1:48
McDONNELL-DOUGLAS AV-8B HARRIER

Tools and materials

Cements

I use two types of liquid cement. The first is Revell Contacta, which is deposited onto the kit in small droplets, allowing you to control the volume of cement reaching the parts. I also use EMA Plasticweld: this is very much like Tennax 7R (which is no longer sold in the UK). You fill the mating areas with cement then hold together until set, usually within about 10 seconds. This allows you to get a good join on what can often be poorly fitting kit parts.

I often use tube cement, which give a solid construction. The trick is to apply just enough cement to get a good bond without it being squeezed everywhere. The same can be said for two-part epoxy resin cement, which is used for fixing metal or resin parts to kits. This comes in two parts, adhesive and hardener, that require mixing together before use. It gives a good solid bond but allows you time to check alignment unlike cyanoacrylate (superglue), which acts instantly.

Fillers

A favourite of mine is Revell Plasto. This filler sets quickly and does not shrink or crumble when sanded. An alternative is Squadron Green Stuff.

Tools

A key tool essential for good modelling is a saw. This was used for removing the nose for the Sea Harrier model. It is also useful when removing casting lugs from resin parts too.

Paints
Primers

For a cheap and simple alternative to modelling paints, you can use car paint from your local auto store. I use grey primer but white is also suitable. When applied over a model, ensure there is no trace of enamel paint as the two don't mix. Grey primer gives a good overall finish to a model, showing up joints or

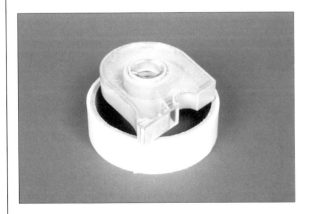

Two types of masking tape: yellow modelling masking tape from Tamiya (on top), and standard decorating masking tape. The Tamiya tape is good for crisp sharp masking along demarcation lines, canopy frames and camouflage whilst the standard tape is good for overall masking of larger areas – it is a much cheaper item to buy.

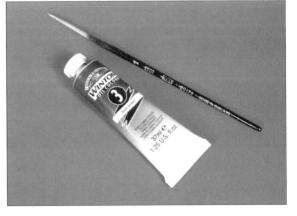

For a weathering wash you can use oil paint, thinned with white spirit. Burnt Umber makes an excellent colour for a wash on a model as it adds just the right tone. I shy away from using black for a wash as I feel it would create too strong a contrast. (GA)

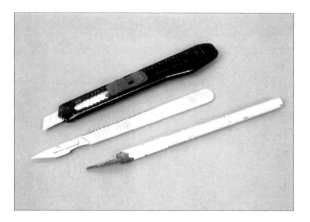

ABOVE A sample of modelling knives used. At the top is a retractable knife used for general modelling. Below that a scalpel used for finer cutting. Bottom is an old X-Acto knife used for applying filler and working things such as paint used on dioramas.

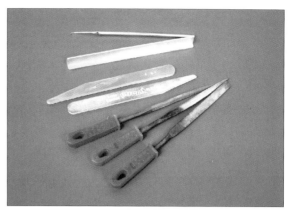

ABOVE As well as knives, a selection of files and sanding/scribing aids are useful. The Squadron scriber at the top is used for replacing panel lines. Below is an Aeroclub Tee-Al sanding plate along with sanding sticks. (GA)

Various types of cement. Revell liquid cement, Italeri tube cement and Araldite two part epoxy, vital for things such as resin parts. (GA)

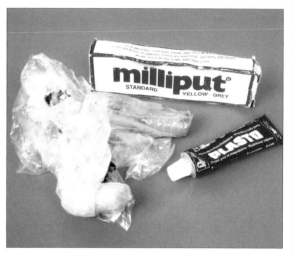

Filler is vital nowadays for filling gaps. Milliput is a two-part filler that sets like rock, while the Plasto is a finer filler. (GA)

other errors that will require correction. It also gives you a uniform colour over which to paint. You can paint enamel over acrylic, but not vice versa.

The 1/72-scale P.1127 I built was finished in primer before being sprayed with a metallic silver auto paint. This gave me a nice metallic silver finish and it dries much quicker than standard model paints. Make sure you have good ventilation when using such materials.

Oil paint

Some modellers use enamels and acrylics as a wash when weathering models. I often use artists' oil paints, which work well too. These can be thinned using white spirit and run along panel lines. After leaving them for a while, the excess can then be wiped off, leaving traces in any recesses, which gives depth to a model. You should really seal your model with a coat of gloss varnish before using oil paints just to ensure no damage is caused to the model paints or decals.

Modelling the Harrier in 1/72

In this chapter we will look at how to take an older kit and bring it up to modern standards – as well as covering an early Harrier type. By using some aftermarket products and a bit of work with Plasticard, as well as cleaning up the kit parts, a decent replica can be produced. I have always felt the modeller has to be three things – engineer, artist and illusionist. Engineer, in actually getting the model constructed in an acceptable way; artist, by skillfully replicating the colour scheme and finish worn by the aircraft; and illusionist, in presenting your own individual concept of how you feel the aircraft looked.

The Airfix P.1127 kit

The subject selected is the 'old man' of the Harrier family, the P.1127. The original Airfix kit dates back to 1962. Dropped by Airfix for a number of years the kit became a real collector's item, often fetching a high price for a mint condition kit. In the last couple of years Airfix have seen fit to re-issue it, pretty much as it was 40 years ago but with updated decals. Good references are vital as a preliminary part of the project. *Harrier, The Vertical Reality* by Roy Braybrook contains excellent colour photos of the Hawker P.1127/Kestrel.

Basic preparation

There are a good number of modellers who would simply pass over a kit of this vintage, basic as it is. On opening the box you are met by a fairly simple kit in grey plastic, with a little bit of flash showing the age of the moulds. Spending a few minutes cleaning up the parts will reveal just where the modeller needs to do some work, the cockpit being the main area. The kit features raised detail on the fuselage but thankfully it pre-dates the infamous 'Airfix Riveteer' that plagued kits later in the 1960s.

When removing kit parts from the sprue always use cutters rather than just pulling the parts loose. This prevents the parts from being damaged. Any excess

The Airfix 1/72 P.1127 kit. (GA)

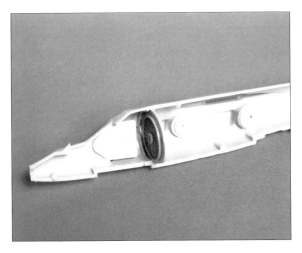

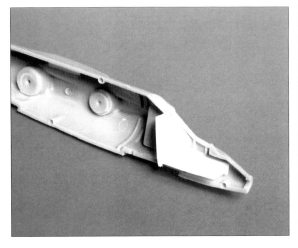

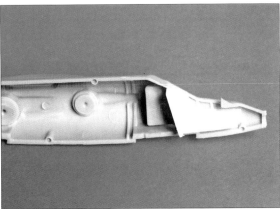

ABOVE LEFT The interior of the Airfix P.1127 is very basic to say the least, but common for kits now 40 years old. Here the intake plates and engine front have been cemented in place before cockpit scratchbuilding begins. Also the locating mounts for the exhaust nozzles have been cemented in. (GA)

ABOVE RIGHT, AND LEFT A basic rear bulkhead and floor were added first to the interior of the kit. These are made from 15 thou plastic card obtained from any decent model shop. It is cut roughly to size then, after being cemented in, is trimmed to fit. After the floor and rear bulkhead I added side consoles from plasticard. These were a simple shelf-type top with side panels added afterwards, and trimmed to fit. Simple interiors like this don't take long to produce. Also framework has been added to the cockpit sides. (GA)

plastic can then be cleaned up by use of a modelling knife, wet and dry sandpaper, or a sanding stick. Only remove the parts you intend to use at the time: this saves smaller parts from getting lost.

Many older kits may suffer from moulding deficiencies such as sink marks or excess plastic: this is due to the age of the moulds. Sink marks can be filled with a touch of filler, and then sanded smooth. Any excess plastic can be carefully removed with light sanding. Many older kits also feature raised rivet detail which is often over-scale and detracts from the model. I tend to use Aeroclub sanding mats to clean up areas such as wings and fuselages as these leave a smoother, more even finish.

Once you have cleaned up the basic parts you should always wash them in warm soapy water, rinse them and leave them to dry naturally. I use an old toothbrush to work into any engraved panel lines or 'hard to get to' places. Also washing the parts removes any traces of mould release agent that sometimes can be found on kits. This leaves the kit with a greasy feel to it and paint will not adhere to any unclean areas.

Cockpit detailing

Another area that often puts modellers off older kits is the lack of detail in the cockpit. Very few old kits have resin or etched brass sets available to create instant off-the-shelf interiors, and the P.1127 is no exception. Now, you may say why not simply use an etched set? Well, the P.1127 was a late 1950s vintage prototype and a modern state of the art etched cockpit update set would not look correct. Also, it will have been designed for another kit and this would cause trouble in fitting.

After the rest of the basic assembly was completed the nose probe was added to the model. This was not a good fit and required filling and sanding down more than once. Here it has been sanded down prior to a coat of primer. Work is still needed on the wing/fuselage joints. (GA)

So what's the answer? Simple, a bit of basic scratchbuilding. Most model shops will carry a stock of Plasticard in different thicknesses. I tend to use either 10 or 15 thou for cockpit detailing.

Splitter plates are placed into the P.1127 fuselage, and now we can add a basic floor from Plasticard before building a pair of simple side consoles. These are just basically shelves running along the cockpit sides boxed in to the floor with another piece of Plasticard. As the P.1127 was a prototype the interior would not have been as complex as that of a later production aircraft. Switch panels can be made from plastic strip detailed with switches made from small pieces of stretched sprue, or even raided from other etched brass frets. In 1/72 scale you can easily create the illusion of a detailed cockpit with minimal cost and effort.

The Harrier family has always featured a prominent throttle control on the left console. Cutting a section of plastic rod to fit, then slicing it into a 'D' section can reproduce this. When attached to the console, you have a ready-made throttle quadrant, which only needs some throttle levers – provided by sprue.

Now you have the basics in place, all you need to add are a seat, instrument panel and control column. The control column can be one taken from the spares box or made from a piece of plastic rod. You can also make an instrument panel from Plasticard or do as I did and raid a panel from an etched set, cut down to fit.

Now it comes to painting the interior. During the late-1950s and early-1960s, aircraft interiors were usually painted black, so that was the colour I applied to the interior of the kit. Once dry I, dry-brushed the interior with silver to highlight the details.

The Airfix kit comes with the standard pilot figure and a seat more akin to a deck chair – certainly not a suitable candidate for an ejection seat. You can spend time making one from scratch if you like – or take an easier way.

White metal parts

For the last 20 years Aeroclub have produced a range of white-metal ejector seats for many different aircraft. Now you don't want an up-to-date Martin-Baker Mk.9 seat, as this would be historically incorrect. I opted for an earlier Mk.3 as fitted to the Hawker Hunter, the reason being that both aircraft were built by Hawker and, at the time of the P.1127, the Hunter was a current front-line aircraft.

The seats come with very little cleaning up required. I usually give them a quick blast of grey primer, just to give a good key to paint on. The basic seats should be painted black with dark green seat cushions. I highlighted the detail by dry-brushing the cushions and seat straps with a lighter shade of green and used silver to highlight the seat details. When finished the seat was secured in place using two-part epoxy resin cement.

Dry-brushing

Dry-brushing is a good way of highlighting any raised details on kit parts and is a very simple technique to learn. You simply need to use a lighter shade of the same colour; or in the case of the ejector seat use silver as it gives a metallic look to the highlighting.

Simply dip your brush into the paint, then wipe most of it off onto a piece of kitchen roll leaving the minimum amount on the brush. Flicking the brush across the part leaves only the lightest amount on the areas of the part standing proud. But be careful not to apply too much paint.

Construction

With the interior completed the fuselage was assembled with tube cement giving a strong, permanent joint, and left aside to dry. I now turned my attention to the wings, which were cleaned up, and using a scribing tool I improved the engraved flap detail. The kit detail is somewhat poorly defined and by rescribing along the flap lines a crisper effect is obtained.

Next the wings were attached to the fuselage using Plasticweld as it sets very quickly giving a good, strong joint. It is better to use this type of fast-acting liquid cement on poorly fitting parts as these can basically be 'welded' into the correct position. This saves difficulties over trying to align ill-fitting parts with slow setting cement.

Having left it all to set for a couple of hours, I then applied filler over all of the joints. When the filler had set, the kit was sanded down and the joints checked. I opted now to build XP836 with the longer nose probe and straight tail. The kit gives options for a bullet fairing on the tail and the shorter nose. As the kit gives decal options for 836 and 831 check your references to ensure that your choice of markings and aircraft configuration match. This is where the use of reference books and magazine articles is vital, as these prototype aircraft underwent numerous changes during development.

The longer nose is a rather poor fit with a large step where it meets the fuselage – so out with the filler once again. When trying to update a kit of this vintage there are no short cuts.

Scribing detail

One area of the P.1127 that needed some help was the fin/rudder area. The wing flaps are engraved but the rudder is indicated by a raised line, a faint one at that. I simply laid a steel rule along the rudder line and scribed a line using the correct scribing tool. A quick clean up with a little wet'n'dry removes the raised detail leaving a nice neat scribed rudder line.

Preparing to paint

Once the construction is completed the entire model is washed in warm soapy water again. Once dry it is time to apply a primer coat. Priming models gives an even base on which to paint, and it shows any flaws that require further attention. If you chose to use an acrylic paint you can't apply it over enamel paints, so ensure there are no traces of enamel. Also, cockpits need to be masked off if the canopies are not in place, as well as other openings such as wheel wells.

Another good reason for priming your models is that if you have used, say, a resin conversion set that is moulded in a different colour to the kit, you will have

ABOVE The P.1127 kit features no real rudder as this is only shown by a line of rivets running down the fin. These rivets need to be sanded down and a rudder line needs to be scribed in the correct place. (GA)

ABOVE This image shows the newly scribed rudder line. The fin has also been sanded down to remove the over-scale rivet detail. (GA)

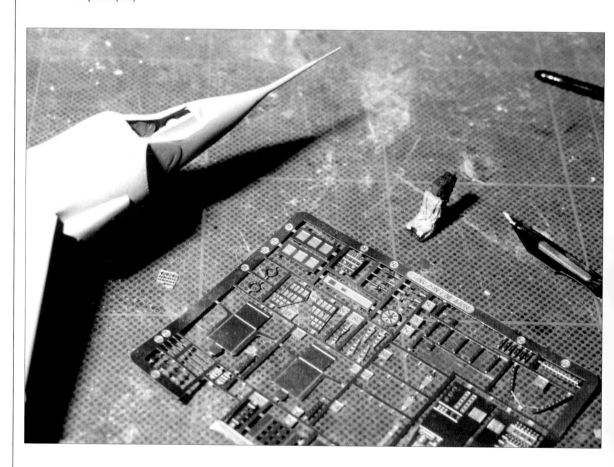

With basic construction completed it's time to set about adding cockpit detail to the P.1127. An Aeroclub white metal seat was used to replace the 'deckchair' included in the kit. Interior details in the shape of instrument panel and console details came from old etched brass sets in the spares box. (GA)

a single colour base rather than trying to cover two contrasting colours. Also some resins resent the modeller trying to put enamel paint onto them, so a coat of primer gives you a key to which you can apply your paint.

Canopies and clear bits

Canopies and other clear parts are often considered problem areas for modellers. The P.1127 canopy is a single-piece item that is not the greatest example of its type. The frame lines were almost impossible to make out and the fit left much to be desired. The trick I use is to mix up a small amount of epoxy resin cement. It gives a strong joint, and does not fog canopies as Superglue does. I applied some along the base of the canopy and attached it to the model. This was left to set leaving a few small gaps visible where the canopy did not meet the model. To fill these gaps I apply Krystal Kleer along the joint and then wipe off any excess using a damp finger. Once dry you have a tidy sealed canopy ready to mask.

Silver finishes

Another area that sends modellers running is trying to create natural metal or silver finishes. One simple option is to use an aerosol car paint. This can give a good finish: for older aircraft in aluminium dope or painted silver finish, a non-metallic type can easily be found. When spraying these ensure good ventilation of the area: also, make sure the paint goes on wet, i.e. don't spray from so far away that the paint is almost dry when it hits the model or you will have a very poor surface finish. The benefit of using such paints is that they dry very quickly, ready for a quick coat of gloss varnish before decals can be applied. For a more advanced and thoroughly rewarding way of achieving an NMF, see the images on the following pages.

The completed cockpit with detail added, and a new Aeroclub seat: the interior was painted black before being highlighted with silver to add a little depth to it. The kit canopy has been cleaned up before being fitted to the model, prior to painting. The added weight of white metal seats also helps the stability of models giving them a little extra ballast. These accurate yet inexpensive seats add a lot to the finished model. (GA)

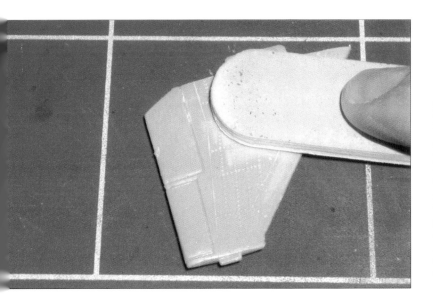

Stage 1 of creating a top-class NMF on the P.1127 – preparation. There's no difference here to when you decorate the walls at home – preparation is everything when trying to create a realistic 'silver' finish. The P.1127 is a very old kit indeed and as was the fashion about 40 years ago, the prominent raised rivet detail needs to be removed. A nail polisher is ideal as is wet and dry paper, used wet. 600 grade should do, finishing with 1200 grade. (GC)

Stage 2: cyano glue is just superb for filling joins and seams. It dries rock hard and can easily be sanded – you need never see another join line again! To speed up drying time, apply some activator such as that supplied by Ripmax and Sylmasta. The activator sets the glue immediately and in a few minutes the affected area can be sanded. (GC)

Stage 3: once the coarser side of your nail polisher or wet and dry has been completed, the area should be polished. The nail buffer is ideal for this – usually having three different polishing surfaces on each stick. Remember – any blemish at all will show up when it comes to spraying your 'silver' paint. (GC)

Stage 4: having got rid of all the surface detail, now is the time to replace any new detail you want. A pounce wheel-riveting tool is handy. You can get these from any good tool supply company such as Shesto and Micromark. A straight edge is essential and a steel rule works well or try using different widths of labelling tape (like Dymo tape) for curved areas. This tape is excellent for using with an Olfa P-Cutter too when rescribing new panel lines. (GC)

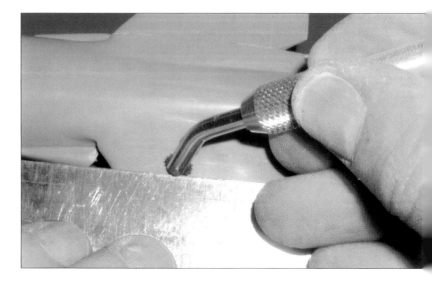

Stage 5: by gently rubbing graphite pencil dust into the newly riveted area, your handiwork shows up: any errors or missed areas can be addressed by filling with cyano and starting that small section again. (GC)

Stage 6: an acrylic grey primer, like the ones used for priming in vehicle repairs, is ideal at this point. Alclad II is being used in this process, and priming is essential when using this paint medium. A tip here is to go easy on the spraying – the paint comes out at a high pressure and it's easy to flood all your lovely new detail and lose it. Try gently ghosting – a little paint sprayed in many light coats, dusted or ghosted onto the surface. (GC)

Stage 7: now it's time to start spraying your chosen colours from the Alclad II range. You can of course try other paints – the Humbrol Metalcote range is also excellent, but the sheer range of tones now available in the Alclad II collection makes them an ideal choice. The paint comes well thinned and you need to have your airbrush nozzle turned right down so that it's almost closed. Again, as with the primer, just ghost on light coats, leaving a few minutes in between each application. (GC)

Stage 8: All three tones have been applied, and now comes the interesting part – weathering. The best materials to use for this are pencil graphite dust and artist's pastel chalks. The dust is applied using a cotton bud – always remember to add a little and keep on adding in several stages so that you gradually build up the final effect you're looking for. The finish is also smooth enough to take your decals, which is great news. If you want, you can apply a thin coat of satin acrylic varnish like that supplied by Polyscale just to seal in your decals. This rarely affects the nice metallic finish you have created – again, good news. (GC)

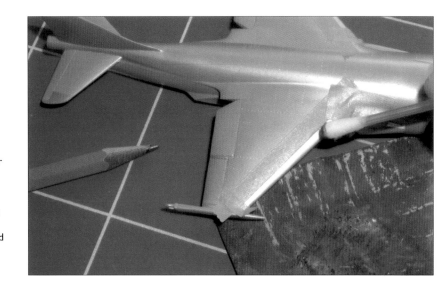

RIGHT AND ABOVE RIGHT
These two pictures show the final finish, just before applying the decals. Note the differing tones and how the rivets just stand out from the rest of the airframe. The lines of rivets are slightly accentuated using pencil graphite applied with a very narrow dry brush. Finally, don't forget to weather the decals once you've applied them – they need to look painted on and part of the aircraft, not an afterthought. (GC)

Decals

This is another area where modellers can make common errors or end up rushing the job. It is an area where you often need to check the references for the particular aircraft you are building. Airfix include a very comprehensive decal sheet in this kit with two options. Referring to the photos in various books I opted to recreate XP836 as shown in one photograph just before it crashed. Airfix include underwing serials and fin flashes as well as black/white reference markings used on the prototypes. These were not on the aircraft at the time of the photograph but quite possibly at a later date.

When applying decals take your time and always apply to a gloss finish or you will get what is called 'silvering' showing through. This is light reflected through where the decal is not seated when applied to a matt finish.

I have always used Micro Sol and Set, or Super Sol/Set as they are now called, which give a wet surface to slide the decal onto and causes a reaction where the decal wrinkles up before settling down to the model. Once dry wipe off excess solution with a damp cloth before sealing with varnish.

BELOW Three views of a finished P.1127, XP836. If you don't have the confidence (or the patience!) to try out the kind of top quality NMF shown opposite, you can still achieve good results using simpler finishing techniques. But, nothing ventured, nothing gained – so why not try it next time? (GA)

1/72 Harrier gallery

Of course there are many other 1/72 Harrier building and finishing options beyond the one that we have focused on in this chapter. The images that accompany this section feature a variety of types and kits created by Harrier fan Tony O'Toole: the aim is to provide modelling inspiration for a variety of Harrier types and variants, and different colour schemes.

ABOVE A 1/72 Harrier T.8 of 899 Naval Air Squadron Royal Navy, based at Yeovilton, wearing the new trainer scheme of all-over gloss black. The model was built from the Heritage Aviation Resin kit and the decals were made up from the spares box with a hand painted 'flying fist' on the tail. This model has been placed alongside another overall black naval aircraft, this being a Hawk T.1 of the Fleet Requirements And Direction Unit, built using an Italeri kit and Modelart decals. (TO)

MIDDLE This model is a Harrier GR.3 of RAF No.4 (IV) Sqn that was built using the very good 1/72 ESCI kit. The decals came with the kit and feature a brightly coloured tail that was painted in the squadron colours. This was part of an initiative in RAF Germany at the time, where the tails of fast jets were painted in bright colours to try to make low-flying aircraft more visible, thereby preventing mid-air collisions, of which there had been a lot at the time. (TO)

BOTTOM Another of Heritage Aviation's resin Harrier trainers in 1/72 scale, this time an earlier Harrier T.4N of 899 Naval Air Squadron in the scheme used in the mid-eighties to late-nineties of overall Dark Sea Grey, which was introduced to the Sea Harrier fleet soon after the Falklands War. The decals for this model came from Modeldecal sheet number 75. (TO)

ABOVE Two models of British second generation Harriers in 1/72 scale. The light grey model is a Harrier GR7 in the temporary light grey ARTF (Alkaline Removable Temporary Finish) colour scheme that was introduced for operations over Northern Iraq in 1992, from Incirlik in Turkey. It was painted over the normal green scheme and was simply washed off when the aircraft ended their detachment but, as can be seen, this paint tended to wear off whilst in use. The second model is of a Harrier T.10 of 20(R) Squadron which is the RAF`s Harrier Operational Conversion Unit (OCU) based at RAF Wittering. This squadron replaced the original training unit 233 OCU but it continues to wear the colours and the Welsh Wildcat head badge of the old unit on the tail of its aircraft. The model shown here is wearing the original two-tone green low level scheme that was worn by the second generation Harrier force initially, but this was replaced in the late 1990s by a two-tone grey scheme to suit its now more prevalent medium altitude role. Both kits are by Airfix. (TO)

A 1/72 model of a two-seater Harrier TAV-8B trainer of the United States Marine Corps in the markings of their training unit VMAT 203 which is based at Cherry Point in the USA. The kit is an old one by Italeri but the markings are from the latest release of the Harrier T10/ TAV-8B by Airfix and feature some sort of special marking on the tail. The model also wears the current F-16 type three-tone grey colour scheme used by the US Marine Corps Harrier IIs. (TO)

ABOVE Another model of a Harrier T.4N of 899 NAS, but this time wearing a light grey scheme. The colour is actually Medium Sea Grey, which is worn by the current Sea Harrier FA2 force, but this is the only two-seat trainer known to have worn the scheme. The aircraft crashed shortly after receiving this scheme, but at the time was wearing a set of wings from an RAF Harrier which carried the Dark Sea Grey and Dark Green disruptive camouflage worn by that service's first generation aircraft. The model itself is a heavily converted old Heller Bobcat kit with many parts added to it and the decals were all from the spares box, using a couple of old photographs from magazines as reference material. (TO)

A strange subject – a Harrier GR.3 in use by the Royal Navy. It is in fact in use by 899 NAS at Yeovilton and is used to help train maintenance crews who are going on to serve with the Sea Harrier fleet, hence the letters ETS on the side, which stand for Engineering Training School. It is painted like a Sea Harrier to help add realism to their training, but obviously its flying days are over. The Royal Navy actually uses quite a few Harrier GR.3s in the ground-training role, from use in engineering training to teaching new aircraft handlers how to move Sea Harriers around the deck of an aircraft carrier, using a concrete apron at Culdrose in Cornwall instead of a ship. The model shown here is built straight from the box and is by Hasegawa in 1/72 scale with the decals coming from the spare's box. This aircraft has recently been featured on an aftermarket decal sheet by SKY from Italy on their sheet number 72-044. (TO)

Modelling the Harrier in 1/48

In this section we will examine key areas related to tackling the Harrier in 1/48 scale, and we'll also take the modelling to a more advanced stage. We'll look at adding detail to a cockpit and seat from scratch, adding figures, applying weathering, exhaust stains and adding dirt to the underside of the aircraft, and detailing the Harrier's undercarriage.

Airfix 1/48-scale Harrier GR.3

The kit chosen to demonstrate these key detailing techniques is the Airfix 1/48-scale Harrier GR.3. By now fairly old, the kit is quite good overall, but in places is a little basic: with the help of some TLC, key areas can be significantly improved. Let's start with the cockpit area first – especially important if you want to display your finished model with the canopy open.

In the 'office'

The cockpit area on 1/48-scale and larger scale kits is an area where you can add plenty of detail. You can choose to purchase resin after-market sets to do the job – or you can employ a little scratchbuilding. Starting with the sidewalls, the internal framework can be added using plastic strip. The instruments can be made from plastic strip and stretched sprue switches and built onto sections of plastic strip that can then be added into the cockpit. The instrument panel can be built up in a similar way and simply slotted into place. Dials can be added from a specialist etched set, such as those from Reheat or Airwaves, or by using a drill or punch and die set. This is a good way to learn about scratch-building detail and a way of advancing your modelling skills. The throttle lever can be made by using a D-shaped piece of plastic rod: scribe the grooves for the levers into the throttle unit. The levers themselves can be made by using plastic rod or stretched sprue.

The images on the pages that follow will hopefully provide more ideas and tips for getting some fine results.

The ejector seat can be tricky – but you can add the side detail from plastic strip or rod giving you quite an effective seat. Straps can be made using strips of masking tape and etched brass seat buckles. You need to cut strips of tape about 1–2mm wide. Lay the tape out on glass or a piece of thick Plasticard, and using a sharp blade and steel rule you can easily cut suitable strips. Then loop these through the buckles and build up the seat belt arrangement. You can anchor these in place with dabs of superglue.

ABOVE Airwaves' etched brass set.

BELOW The cockpit parts supplied with the Airfix Harrier GR.3 have to be the main weakness in the kit – they are very basic indeed. The kit seat hardly represents the Martin Baker Mk.9L fitter in the GR.3 – so I decided to scratch build a new seat (see page 24) (GC)

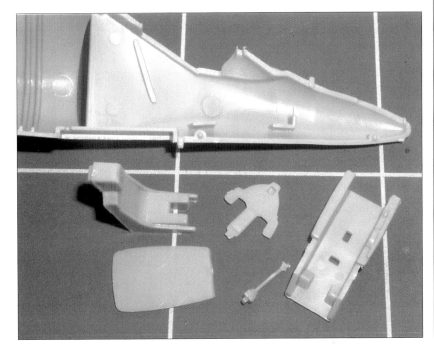

Detailing the cockpit tub is one of the things I enjoy most about modelling jet aircraft. Invariably there are aftermarket etched metal sets available but not in this case – for the GR.3 at least. Airwaves do a set for the Royal Navy FRS.1 but the detail is different. Here you can see that small instrument dials and bezels are being used (from the Reheat range). Much extra detail is going in using scrap pieces of brass from the spares box and the rear of the tub is being completely reworked. The gun sight arrangement is where you need to do a lot of work to obtain a realistic outcome. (GC)

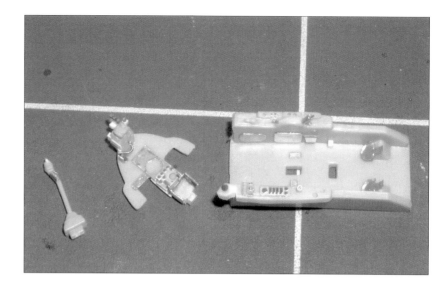

The left fuselage half has plenty of formers and riggers added using different pieces of plastic strip. Additionally lead foil and brass wire help to add the remaining detail. Note here how the area where the cockpit tub has been marked out with pencil so that you don't get any horrible snags and obstructions when the tub is finally mated to the fuselage halves. (GC)

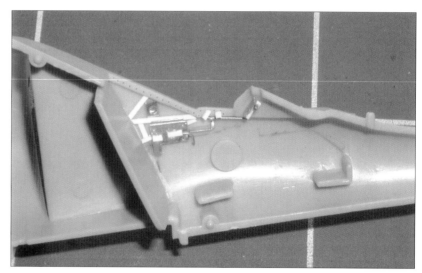

The right side of the fuselage this time. There really is no substitute for good quality reference photographs of the cockpit and these are not always easy to come by. The IPMS Harrier SIG website (see the reference section at the end of the book for the address) has some good photographs. Note too in this photo the small rivet detail along the cockpit sill. This is achieved using a hand-held pin vice drill and 0.3mm drill bit. (GC)

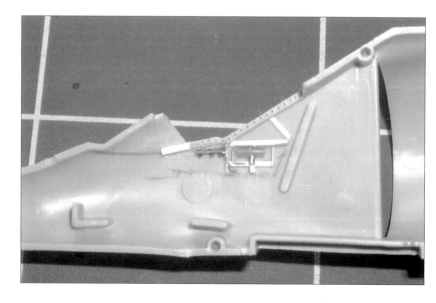

There are several ways that you can obtain a realistically weathered cockpit. Here I have used the pre-shading technique. This simply involves spraying the whole cockpit and any sub-assemblies dark grey. Make sure to get into all the small corners so that everything is covered. (GC)

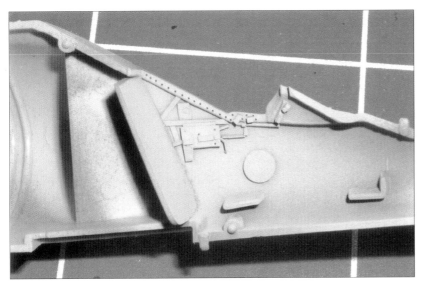

Once the dark grey is dry the main cockpit colour can be ghosted on – in this case, Medium Sea Grey. By ghosting I mean spraying very light coats of the Medium Sea Grey over the base coat. Make sure you keep the airbrush head at 90 degrees to the surface so that the light grey goes on flat against the surface. This allows the darker grey to show around the edges and shadows to appear, as you can see in this picture. The idea is to create a 3D effect. (GC)

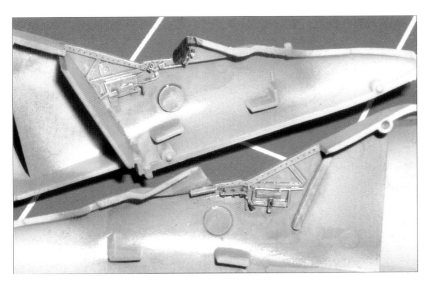

The next stage in the process is to give the whole cockpit a wash – and for this I invariably use Tamiya Smoke (X-19). It is a really brilliant colour – being a dirty gloss clear varnish that collects into all the corners and detail you've added. The detail here appears to 'pop out' at you and I feel this is just what I'm after. Note the two large circles on the fuselage sides. These are moulding marks left by the moulds when the parts are extracted during the injection-moulding process. There is no great need to remove them, as they sit below the side instrument consoles and out of view when the tub is attached to the fuselage. (GC)

RIGHT The completed cockpit tub seen from the rear left side. The final effect is pleasing. The actual instrument dials came from an old decal sheet – cut out and placed according to the photographs I have. They are a bit lighter than on the real GR.3 but I wanted them to be at least visible in the final cockpit, which is very small in quarter scale. Again, note the wash that has collected in the corners and around the detail. The gun sight just needs a small piece of acetate to simulate the Head Up Display (HUD). This is best done at the end of the whole project so as to avoid damage. The pilot's rolling map display seen here in green is achieved by painting the interior of the circle silver and filling in with Tamiya clear green on top. Not 100 per cent authentic but it looks more interesting as a result. (GC)

MIDDLE The completed cockpit tub seen from the right side this time. The canvas boot at the foot of the control column is painted Tamiya Buff (XF-57) and washed with Citadel Ink Skaven Brown. A final dry-brushing of the part with a very light brown gives a realistic finish. (GC)

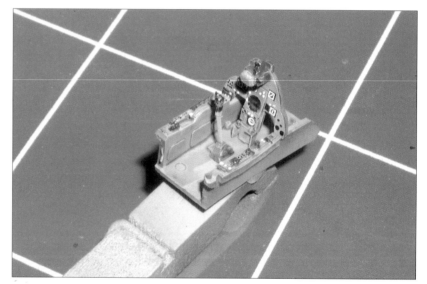

BOTTOM This is my attempt at scratch-building the Martin Baker Mk.9L ejection seat. It took a long time and has 108 parts! A little obsessive, perhaps – but it looks the part when installed in the finished aircraft. Plastic card (main seat), Blu-Tack (cushions on seat and headrest), lead foil (seat harness) and fuse wire account for the main components. Small buckles and belt fittings came from an old Reheat etched-metal set. (GC)

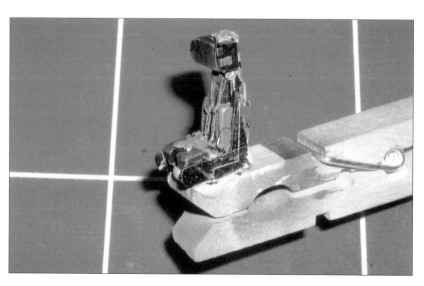

Weathering

Weathering your model consists of applying an overall dirty wash to tone down the scheme and markings, giving an 'in-service' look to the completed model. Metallic washes can be added to the undercarriage in a similar way. Another aspect worth noting is that the Harrier is notorious for the streaming exhaust stains running down the rear fuselage. In addition, because the Harrier operates in rough field conditions, mud splashes (where the aircraft has taxied over fields) and paint chip damage can add that authentic touch.

Paint chipping

The immaculate schemes applied to brand new aircraft are very soon lost once the aircraft begins actually flying. Varying weather conditions or everyday knocks can cause chipping to the paint surface, in a similar way to the average motor vehicle with stone chips on the front end.

You can apply these chips with a small brush just dabbing or touching into various areas. This is usually on areas exposed to airflow and any debris thrown into the path of an aircraft. Using a small brush touched into some aluminium paint, touch into the fronts of the intakes, wing and tail leading edges and also areas where ground crews would be removing panels. Practice first on an old kit so you don't spoil your model.

Washes

This does certainly have a dramatic effect on any model. I use oil paint thinned with white spirit for my basic wash. This is run along all of the panel lines, into openings and around any raised parts of the model. Work on small sections at a time. I run the paint into the area worked on and leave it for five minutes. Wipe off the excess using a piece of kitchen towel, working from front to back as per the airflow over an aircraft. This will smear a brown streaky finish all over the model.

Now take a clean piece of towel, apply some clean thinner to it with a brush and wipe again. Most of the oil paint will come off but you may have to wipe a few times to get a finish where the dirty wash remains in the engraved areas or around the raised parts. For getting into tight corners, a cotton bud/swab is useful. Gradually work your way round the model until you have the finish you desire. Leave the model aside overnight to dry out completely.

Chipped paint can be added to the intakes or exposed areas of a model by carefull application using silver paint and a brush. Here the intakes of an Airfix GR.3 are getting the treatment. Although silver may seem a bright colour, you can tone it down when applying a wash to your model at a later stage. (GA)

How to apply a weathering wash. Here the Airfix GR.3 is shown prior to application of the wash paint. (GA)

The paint is applied over the panel detail with a brush. It is applied slightly thinned with white spirit and then left for a while. (GA)

Here the clean-up has begun with the paint wiped off using paper tissue. Note the heavy streaking, which will be further cleaned up. The cotton bud/swab is handy for getting into tight corners. (GA)

Metallic washes

Areas such as the undercarriage, and on other aircraft engines, can be given a metallic wash to highlight detail and add some depth to their finish. For instance, if an aircraft leaks oil or other fluids it tends to take on its own appearance, unlike a normal wash. Take a look at a dirty car engine, for example.

To produce this type of effect, useful on the Harrier's undercarriage legs and outriggers, simply thin down some gunmetal paint so it has a consistency more like water. Apply small amounts using a small brush and let the capillary effect run the paint around the parts, giving depth to their appearance.

Mud, muck and exhaust stains

Aircraft such as the Harrier often operate on unprepared, rough fields, which means they attract considerable dirt. With the undercarriage located so close to the ground, dirt is thrown up onto the aircraft. Drive any vehicle through mud or puddles and dirt will accumulate on the tyres: the same happens with the Harrier. You can apply this by carefully building up dry-brushed, earth-coloured paint onto the tyres. This can be done in stages until you get the level of finish you want.

Mud splashes are slightly different. Dirt will be thrown up onto the underside of the fuselage, and very slightly around the outriggers. Use a larger brush loaded with some thinned down earth-coloured paint. Then using a toothpick, flick the paint from the front aft of the undercarriage to obtain a suitable effect.

Take a look at any Harrier in front-line service and you will notice the very dark heavy exhaust staining that affects the lower rear fuselage area. You can add this to your model using artist's pastels applied by brush. It works best applied to a matt finish and can be carefully sealed with a light overspray of matt varnish.

Harrier undercarriage

The Harrier has always possessed a weak spot in terms of the construction of the undercarriage and its subsequent 'sit' when completed. Usually one of the outriggers sits off the ground, or if both outriggers sit correctly then the main undercarriage is left dangling in mid-air. One solution to this problem is to build your model with the nosewheel and outriggers in place, painting and decaling the model before turning to the main undercarriage last of all. Open up the locating hole so the undercarriage legs slide in and out and apply some cement. Ensure the wheels are lined up correctly and gently sit the aircraft down on a flat surface. You can gently adjust the position of the main under-carriage unit so all four undercarriage units sit in unison on the ground. In the images that follow, we'll take a look at adding super detail to the undercarriage area, something that 1/48 scale allows.

As you can see, pictures of the real aircraft undercarriage units are vital if you are going to try and recreate a decent replica in model form. Here you see the nose gear. Key features to note are the two landing/taxi lights – the larger of the two being very prominent; and the multitude of hydraulic and electrical wires around the top of the leg and right side as viewed – note the different thickness of the wires. (GC)

RIGHT AND BELOW LEFT The main gear assembly located centrally under the aircraft is a very sturdy structure – and not easy to photograph. Both front and rear views are included here to help you to see the features. Note: The front view shows the heavy dark brake mechanism attached to the inside of each wheel hub. This is a gunmetal colour in contrast to the Light Aircraft Grey leg. The small main gear door at the front of the wheel well is very thin and best replaced with aluminium foil (from an old drinks can) or thin plasticard. The rear view (shown below) highlights the hydraulic lines and further similar detail in the roof of the wheel well at the gear rotation point. The Remove Before Flight (RBF) tags can add a nice touch to your finished scale model. (GC)

BELOW The Starboard outrigger undercarriage unit. The main details to note here are the hydraulic lines down the upper rear retraction arm and bracing bands around the main forward unit. The small hinge arm connecting the oval forward faring to the forward unit is just visible. In addition, notice the tubular locking device fitted around the bright retraction arm – these are usually bright red in colour and have RBF tags attached. (GC)

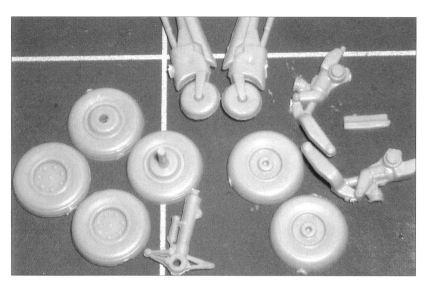

The Airfix undercarriage unit parts are not bad – just simplified. This makes them ideal candidates for the super-detail treatment. As far as they go they're reasonably accurate, although the main wheel hubs have raised detail where holes exist on the actual aircraft. Perhaps just noticeable on the wing tip outriggers are large sinkholes immediately above the wheel. These were filled using cyano glue and sanded flat. (GC)

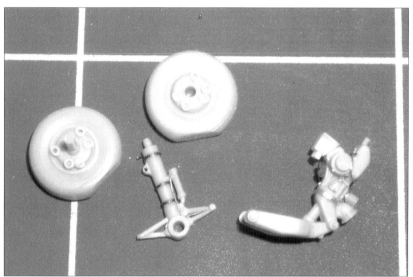

The main gear and nose gear assemblies have been detailed in this shot. The raised round detail on the wheel hubs is represented using small rings cut from plastic tube. Hydraulic lines are fuse wire of various thicknesses. Additional detail, like the metal bands around the main legs, comes from thin strips of lead foil – the sort you find around the neck of decent bottles of wine. All these parts are attached using cyano glue and an activator liquid to set the glue instantly. This is great for speeding up construction. (GC)

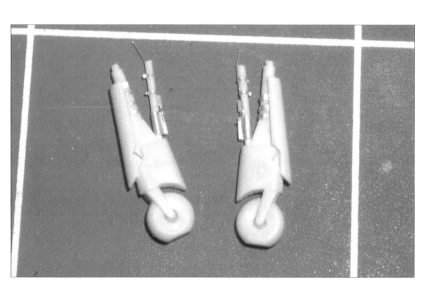

This close-up shot shows the outrigger undercarriage units fully detailed. The hydraulic lines can just be seen, as can the bracing bands from lead foil. The tyres need sanding flat (see the photo of the real aircraft unit on page 27). I have tried to represent the locking devices fitted to the bright retraction arms: as noted before, to finish it all off you could add RBF tags once painting is complete. (GC)

RIGHT The completed assemblies are a far cry from the basic components you started with – but well worth all the extra work. Note here the flattened tyres – a feature of the Harrier GR.3. The legs were painted in gloss enamel (Xtracolor X15 BS627 Light Aircraft Grey) The tyres are best painted a dark grey and not black – which is just too dark to be authentic. A good choice is Humbrol Matt No.67. The grey, when dry, is washed all over with Tamiya acrylic X-19 Smoke. This gets into all the nooks and crannies and gathers around raised detail, much as grime and dirt would. Citadel Colour Rust wash is the brown colour you can see in small quantities around some of the joints. The end result – a nicely weathered finish. (GC)

MIDDLE This close up photo of the nose gear is designed to show the use of two of MVs small lenses (available from ED Models in the UK). These are excellent representations of the real thing and add greatly to the final effect. The smaller of the two lenses is shown yellow in colour here but should be a white lens. The tyres are dry-brushed liberally with light grey pastel chalk dust and this seems to really bring them to life. The new electrical cables and hydraulic lines also stand out. (GC)

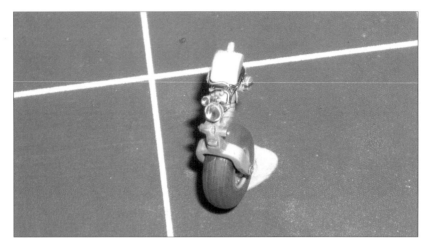

BOTTOM This final photograph in the sequence brings all the completed units together: all that's needed is to attach them to the completed airframe. This is invariably best done right at the end of the finishing process, once the decals have been applied and all the weathering completed. (GC)

Adding crew

Many aircraft modellers shy away from putting figures into models, but adding the kit pilot can bring a lot to your model. Let's look at a quick and simple way to paint the pilot figure from the Airfix box in suitable atire for the GR.3.

I first painted the flying overalls in Humbrol dark green, and left the figure to dry. I ran some darker black-green into the creases and folds of the pilot's flight gear to add depth. When dry, I dry-brushed the original colour over this to pick out the bulk of the colour, leaving darker paint in the shadow areas. Next I highlighted the overalls by dry-brushing light green over them. This gave me three levels of colour depth on the figure. The helmet, mask, gloves and boots are all black: the mask and gloves are made from Neopreen, a type of rubber, and the boots are leather. These were painted satin black before being dry-brushed with medium grey to pick out the highlights.

ABOVE Airwaves' metal figures. (GA)

When it comes to figures, you are not just restricted to the pilot of course. Adding a few ground crew figures to your model setting can be of great benefit. In the photograph below, showing a USMC AV-8B serving with IFOR over the Balkans, I used Airwave's metal figures, which are actually Vietnam War-era figures. The crew chief wears 'popcorn'-type camo gear – basically sand-coloured with medium and dark green patches. First I painted the trousers sand then carefully applied the two greens using a small brush, applying the lighter shade first. His t-shirt was painted bright green before applying flesh to the skin areas. Hair was done in brown with black sunglasses and boots. The second figure is basically an NCO who was painted in full camo gear uniform with an olive drab cap. This figure was painted in a similar way to the other. One difficulty was actually adding depth as painting shadows and highlighting details is not easy on a complex camouflage uniform. So I applied a dark grey thinned wash into the details, which brought the figures to life.

BELOW Adding crew or figures to your display adds a great deal of life to the aircraft, as well as an improved sense of scale. (GA)

ABOVE The basic figure from the Airfix kit painted with Dark Green overalls, before depth is added. (GA)

ABOVE Here you can see the black-green painted into the shadows with dark green dry-brushed over the figure to carefully show the depth of detail in creases and folds. (GA)

The suit has been dry-brushed in light green on the highlights. Also the helmet and face along with other details are now painted. (GA)

The finished figure. With the face mask on, face painting would be a lot easier! (GA)

1/48 Harrier gallery

The following models, created by Tony O'Toole and Piero de Santis, will hopefully they will provide some more options and ideas for you when modelling the Harrier in 1/48 scale. A variety of kits and colour schemes have been selected – thank you, Tony and Piero!

ABOVE The RAF's latest version of the Harrier is the GR.7 which is shortly to be upgraded to the GR9. At the moment there is no kit available in 1/48th-scale of any version of the second generation Harrier in RAF service, and indeed the only kit of any of the second generation Harriers in service worldwide is the quite old Monogram kit. This is the kit that has been used for this model and it has been converted to a British aircraft by lengthening the nose and adding the various lumps and bumps using Milliput and scrap plastic carved to shape. I believe there is a state of the art kit on its way from Hasegawa soon and hopefully a RAF version will be able to be built from it, but there are resin conversion sets for the GR.7 available, designed for the Monogram kit from Maintrack Models and Amraam Line: both unfortunately were unavailable when I built this kit. The decals for this model came from SKY decal sheet 48-028. (TO)

MIDDLE A pre-Falklands Sea Harrier FRS.1 of 800 NAS Royal Navy wearing the pre-war scheme of Extra Dark Sea Grey and White with colourful squadron markings and roundels, which had been the traditional colour scheme for Fleet Air Arm fighters since the early 1960s, first being worn by the Harriers older relative the Hawker Seahawk. The model is the 1/48-scale Tamiya kit and has been built from the box with the addition of scratch built drop down doors on the air intakes, using plastic card for the doors and a pilot from the spares box. (TO)

BOTTOM A very colourful Harrier variant is the AV-8S Matador that was until recently flown by the Spanish Navy. These aircraft have since been sold on to Thailand to operate off that countries new aircraft carrier, being replaced in Spanish service by the newer AV-8B and AV-8B+. This model was built in 1/48 scale from the old Monogram kit, which is still very good but rare, with the decals coming again from SKY of Italy on their sheet 48-028 which is crammed with decals for all sorts of Harriers. (TO)

ABOVE This Sea Harrier FRS.1 is from 899 NAS and is wearing the special markings to celebrate the squadrons 50th anniversary in 1992. Such markings are rare on Royal Navy aircraft, being more common on RAF aircraft, and they were applied over the standard Dark Sea Grey scheme. These markings are included in the recently re-boxed 1/48-scale kit by Airfix, the one used to build this model. The drop-down air intakes doors were cut out and replaced in the drooping position using Plasticard replacements. (TO)

Another 1/48 Sea Harrier, but this time it is the upgraded FA2 version which incorporates state of the art Blue Vixen radar along with the ability to use the AIM 120B AMRAAM missile. It is built from the Airfix kit and is in the markings of the Royal Navy`s training unit, 899 NAS, who, as well as the RAF's 20(R) Sqn, also use single seaters alongside their two seaters. The model was built from the box, the only alteration being the scratch-built air intake doors that have been drooped down, as per the original aircraft when at rest. The model carries two AMRAAMs under the fuselage with two AIM 9M Sidewinders on the outboard stations under the wings, and 100 gallon fuel tanks inboard, although the larger 190 gallon tanks are more usual on the FA2. (TO)

ABOVE A Harrier GR.3 of 233 Operational Conversion Unit, the original RAF Harrier training unit that was based at RAF Wittering. As with the current 20(R) Sqn and the Royal Navy's 899 NAS this unit, as well as using two seat trainers, used a number of single seaters for more advanced training and also for the use of instructors. The model was built from the Airfix kit with the addition of unit markings from SKY Models decal sheet 48-028. (TO)

This model is of a Sea Harrier of 801 Naval Air Squadron, Royal Navy that was based aboard HMS *Invincible* during the 1982 Falklands War. It is painted in the glossy Extra Dark Sea Grey scheme that was applied overall and wears the modified roundels that were converted from the standard red white and blue type by overpainting the white portion with more blue. The model itself is the 1/48 Sea Harrier FRS.1 from Tamiya but with resin air intakes from Heritage Aviation. The kit actually includes decals for this aircraft when it was flown pre-war by 801's squadron commander 'Sharky' Ward, when it wore the Extra Dark Sea Grey and White scheme (see the chapter on 1/24-scale), and these decals were used for all of the markings on this model with the roundels and 001 code being painted over in blue just like the original aircraft. On most Combat Air Patrols the Sea Harriers carried a 1,000lb bomb on the fuselage pylon and most of these were dropped over the airfield at Port Stanley just to 'annoy' the occupying Argentine forces. One of these bombs however was used in the sinking of the Argentine spy trawler the *Narwal*, even though it was dropped too low to explode. (TO)

ABOVE **RAF Harrier GR.3** This is a BAe Harrier GR.3 (serial number XV778 and tail code 16) from the Royal Air Force's No.1 Squadron based at Wittering, during a deployment to Norway for a NATO winter exercise in 1988. This aircraft was camouflaged with a coat of removable white paint over the standard Dark Green colour.

The model is based on the Harrier GR.1/AV-8A Monogram kit that has been modified to become a GR.3 using a resin laser nose and extended tail from Missing Link, and a Martin Baker Mk.9 metal seat from Aeroclub. The above view shows the opened engine access panels with the scratchbuilt Pegasus engine inside. (PDS)

Rear three-quarter view: note the lowered flap position and the exhaust-stain effect on the rear fuselage. (PDS)

ABOVE Starboard view: note the lowered auxiliary upper intakes doors due the gravity effect. The inset detail shows the opened engine access panels and scratchbuilt Pegasus engine. (PDS)

BELOW Port view: note the in-flight refueling probe over the main engine intake and the transponder bulge and antenna under the nose. (PDS)

ABOVE **RN Sea Harrier FRS.1** This is a BAe Sea Harrier FRS.1 (serial number XZ457 and nose code 14) from the Royal Navy's 800 Squadron onboard the carrier HMS *Hermes* during the Falklands War, spring 1982, with a score of four air-kills. This aircraft was entirely camouflaged with a coat of Extra Dark Sea Grey. The model is based on the Harrier GR.1/AV-8A Monogram kit that has been modified to became an FRS.1, using the radar nose and extended tail from the Airfix Sea Harrier FRS.1 kit and a Martin Baker Mk.10 seat from Aeroclub. The above front view shows the white air-kill markings under the canopy and the red FOD guards inside the main engine intakes. (PDS)

Rear view: note the lowered ventral airbrake and the white roundel circle over painted with blue. (PDS)

ABOVE Starboard view: note the red access ladder attached to the nose and the AIM-9L missile under the outboard wing pylon. (PDS)

BELOW Port view: note the 'chipped' silver paint on the removable access panels. No unit markings were displayed during the conflict. (PDS)

ABOVE **RAF Harrier GR.7, No. 4 Squadron Flag Ship**
This is a McDD/BAe Harrier GR.7 (serial number ZG859)
from the Royal Air Force's No.4 Squadron based at Laarbruch,
Germany, in 1994. This aircraft has a black/red tail painted with
a yellow lightning flash. The model is based on the AV-8B

Monogram kit that has been modified to become a GR.7,
using a resin conversion set from Amraam Line. The above
front three-quarter view shows the large wings and the
enlarged LERX surfaces on the wing attachment point.
(PDS)

Rear view: note the ECM/RWR bumps and lumps on the wing tips and
at the rear ventral strake. (PDS)

ABOVE Starboard view: note the inclined tail surfaces and the extended tail cone. (PDS)

BELOW Port view: note the extended in-flight refueling probe over the main engine intake and the new nose housing the FLIR sensor and a pair of ZEUS system's antenna. (PDS)

ABOVE RAF Harrier GR.7, Operation Warden
This is a McDD/BAe Harrier GR.7 (serial number ZD408, tail code WK) from Royal Air Force's No.3 Squadron based at Incirlik, Turkey, in the 1994 Operation Warden over North Iraq. This aircraft has pale pink and blue roundels and no squadron markings. The aircraft was repainted overall in ARTF Grey. This model is based on the AV-8B Monogram kit that has been modified to become a GR.7 using a resin conversion set from Amraam Line. The above front view shows the extra pylon under the wing to carry self-defence missiles. Grey FOD guards with red warning tags are fitted into the main engine intakes. (PDS)

Rear view: note how the 'chipped' grey paint allows the original NATO Green color to show through, and the exhaust-stain effect on the rear fuselage. (PDS)

ABOVE Starboard view: note the extended inboard access ladder under the main engine intake and the US-made cluster bomb under the wing pylon. (PDS)

BELOW Port view: note the 'sitting position' common on all the Harrier versions and the extended in-flight refueling probe over the main engine intake. (PDS)

ABOVE **USMC AV-8B Plus** This is a McDD AV-8B Plus (serial number 164552 tail code 01) from United States Marine Corp's VMA-542, based at Cherry Point, North Carolina, in 2001. This aircraft has hi-viz squadron markings. The model is based on the AV-8B Monogram kit that has been modified to become a Plus, using a resin conversion set from Amraam Line, and a scratchbuilt radar. The above view shows the open nose cone with the radar antenna exposed. Note also the different colours of the Laser Guided Bombs under the wing. (PDS)

Rear view: note the extra chaff-and-flare launcher packages on the upper rear fuselage and the extended tail intake. (PDS)

ABOVE Starboard view: note the extended inboard access ladder under the main engine intake, and the folded-back nose cone. (PDS)

BELOW Port view: note the large wing, the enlarged LERX surfaces on the wing attachment point and the extended in-flight refueling probe over the main engine intake. (PDS)

Modelling the Harrier in 1/24

Airfix 1/24 Royal Navy Sea Harrier FRS.1

The Harrier version to be modelled in following pages is perhaps the best known machine of the Harrier family – the Royal Navy's superb Sea Harrier. The model featured in this chapter originates from the old Airfix Harrier GR.1 kit that was originally released back in 1974.

With the FSR.1, all the parts needed are in the box, and are in plastic. Airfix have updated their old moulds yet again to provide even more extra parts to enable the original Sea Harrier version to be built. Even so quite a bit of cutting and filling is still required! Despite being built using only the parts from the kit, the modelling does incorporate scratch built improvements such as detailing in the rear wheel bay, cockpit and engine as well as the opening up of an engine access panel.

Initial cutting and sanding

The first thing that needs to be done with the Airfix kit is to cut off the Harrier GR.1 nose to enable the new Sea Harrier nose to be fitted. There are no guidelines to follow when cutting, but I suggest sawing along the rearmost panel line in front of the air intakes and then along the along the lip of the fuselage until level with the air intake. The last cut to sever the nose is then made from this point straight across the upper fuselage.

Now that the initial cutting is over, the next task is one that must really be done with any 1/24-scale Airfix Harrier kit and that is de-scaling most of the rivets. To do this it is simply a matter of smearing model filler across all of the parts that carry these rivet holes. The most prone areas are the fuselage halves, wing tips, undercarriage doors, wing centre section, fin and tailplanes. Other parts have some rivets but they are much lighter and easier to sand away, although some, especially on the wings, can be retained. Most actual Sea Harriers have relatively smooth airframes, using flush rivets, with only the odd rivet or two visible in certain lighting conditions and this is why any serious modeller should attempt to try and carry out this tedious task. It is advisable to look at a number of photographs of the actual aircraft to decide to what degree the rivets are dealt with.

Even more tedious (and messier) than applying filler is sanding it off again, but hopefully after one or two sanding and filling sessions the reward should be some nice smooth pieces with just a hint of some rivets showing through.

Some sections of the Harrier airframe such as access panels do have quite deep holes for the quick fittings and these areas should be retained. A scriber was used to restore most of the already moulded recessed panel lines on the model, as these lines are quite prominent on the actual aircraft. Careful use of the scriber will also serve to highlight the smoother surface of the parts.

The completed Airfix Sea Harrier FRS.1. The engine compartment has been opened up and it carries the gloss Extra Dark Sea Grey and White scheme that was worn by the Sea Harrier when it initially came into service. The colourful markings are for 800 Naval Air Squadron (NAS) Royal Navy in 1981 and the model carries two 1,000lb bombs, portraying the fighter-bomber role that the Sea Harrier can carry out. (TO)

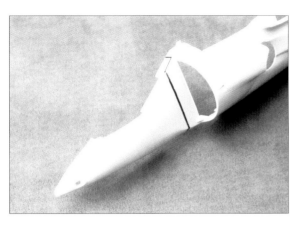

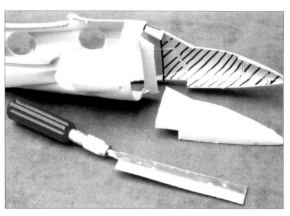

The starting point is to cut off the old Harrier nose. The main reference point is the horizontal panel line that is nearest to the air intake opening. The cut carries straight through to the underside, but stops at the lip of the upper fuselage. When this lip is reached, the cut should be made along it until level with the air intake. From this point a simple cut straight across the fuselage will sever the nose. (TO)

This view shows the nose having been severed using a razor saw, illustrating the amount of plastic that needs to be removed before the model can be started. (TO)

Pre-painting

Now that all of the parts are ready to use, the next stage in building the Sea Harrier is to pre-paint most of the interior pieces on the sprue before they are removed. I find this a much easier method of painting these parts, rather than building up a section and then painting it or removing the individual parts and then fiddling about trying to hold them and paint them. Invariably a little touch up painting is required later to cover up the place where the part was attached to the sprue, but this is easily done later on with less mess. I also find that painting the interior of the model and any engine or cockpit parts at the start of making a model helps to speed up the actual construction, rather than waiting for paint to dry in between the various different stages.

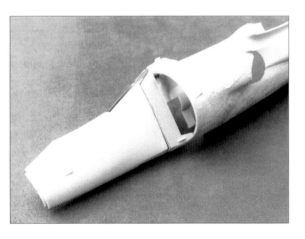

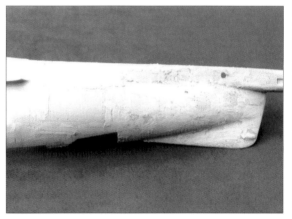

The new Sea Harrier nose section is dry fitted into position to test the fit of the parts. Quite a bit of filler will be needed to blend these different sections together. When fitting the air intakes later, the triangular wedge seen at the bottom of the intake will require cutting off, as this helps them to fit better. Note that the fuselage has been covered with filler. (TO)

Much of the rivet detail is too deep and needs to be de-scaled: Sea Harriers are actually very smooth, as they use flush rivets. The parts of the model most affected are the main fuselage halves, the tailplanes, fin, wing tips and the upper wing centre section. These were covered with model filler, which was then sanded off to provide a smoother finish. Note here with the rear fuselage how the panels are not filled, to retain the rivets. (TO)

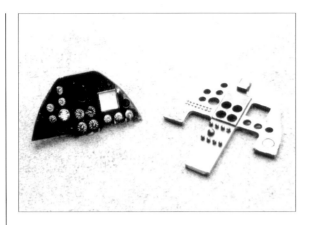

The clever instrument panel comprises two different parts: a clear section for the instruments, and a plastic main panel with holes in it. The rear of the clear part is painted black and the front of each dial is painted gloss white. This white is swiftly rubbed off, cleverly leaving the recessed detail full of white paint to represent the dials. (TO)

When the rear part has been fitted to the instrument panel, the result is a good rendition of the instrument dials. The actual panel itself is a little crude however and needs a little work to improve it. (TO)

Initial construction

As with most models, the first stage of actual construction for this Sea Harrier is the cockpit. The cockpit floor and side walls have already been painted a dark bluey grey, using Polyscale Acrylic Extra Dark Sea Grey, with the side consoles painted Black and Grey with various dials and switches picked out in White, Yellow and Red. All of the detail inside the cockpit was enhanced by dry brushing with white throughout. Dry brushing is a way of highlighting raised detail and is easy to do, with practice, and is very effective. By simply squeezing off most of the paint on a brush, using kitchen towel or similar, until it feels dry and then lightly brushing over any raised detail, the small amount of paint left on the brush will highlight the raised surfaces. This technique however is best learnt using an old model to practice on before being tried out on a relatively expensive Sea Harrier kit.

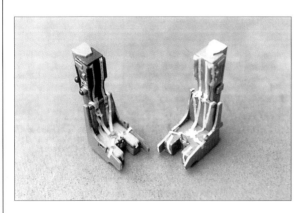

The Martin Baker ejector seat that comes with the Airfix kit is much better than the seat provided in the older Harrier kit, but is still quite basic. To enhance the detail a little, Tamiya modelling tape is cut into strips to create the straps. Small bits of plastic card are added to these for the buckles and the quick-release harness: a tubular section of old sprue is used for the actual quick-release fitting. This picture shows the seat on the right partially painted with the straps being fitted, whilst the one on the left has been finished. (TO)

The assembled cockpit tub, showing the handles for the throttle and engine nozzles on the pilots left-hand console and the addition of extra detailing to the rear bulkhead. This extra detail is made from plastic strip, fuse wire and scrap plastic, and once painted enhances the interior detail considerably. Note also the stitching painted on the straps of the ejector seat. (TO)

One of the parts of this kit that I really like is the instrument panel. Although not over detailed, the actual construction of it is I think really clever. The instruments themselves are part of the clear plastic sprue and the rear part of it should be painted black. Next the protruding dial faces are painted gloss white, but by removing the paint with a finger or cloth straight away, the white paint remains in the recesses to perfectly represent the dials of the instruments. This is then fitted to the instrument panel, which has already been pre-painted, with each instrument fitting into its pre-moulded hole, thereby replicating glass covered instrument dials very well.

The ejection seat of the Sea Harrier kit has been improved upon immensely from the original 1974 kit's seat but some would say that it is still basic. There is in fact an excellent resin seat available from Heritage Aviation, but I elected to try to improve the look of the kit seat, using scratch-building techniques. To do this, after painting the seat in the basic colours of dark grey metalwork with green cushions, sections of Tamiya modelling tape are cut into narrow strips and stuck onto the seat to represent seat straps. To represent buckles small squares of thin plastic card are then added to the tape and for the quick release harness buckles thicker scrap plastic is used with a cylindrical central piece of old sprue representing the quick release fitting. Most of the seat straps can be painted a buff colour, with some in blue and the buckles need to be painted a brassy colour with black centres. To finish off the strap detail a very thin brush is used to make small black dashes on the straps to represent the prominent stitching. Finally the pilot's seat cushion needs painting a sandy colour to represent the lambs wool covers used on the real seats, the head box is painted black and a watercolour wash used to enhance the detail. For the wash I use a mixture of black and raw umber watercolour paints from a tube. A small amount is mixed in a palate and then heavily watered down. The straps of the ejector seat can then be painted over with the watery paint and if done right, most of this should settle on either side of the strap. A wipe with a cloth will remove most of the paint but some will remain next to the strap, serving to give them a little more depth. This technique can be used for other purposes such as highlighting the recessed panel lines on a painted model or to 'dirty up' an area such as the inside of an undercarriage

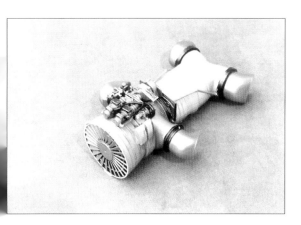

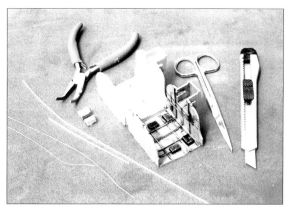

In the Airfix kit, a decent replica of the Rolls Royce Pegasus engine, which makes the Harrier family so special, is provided. The nozzles actually move all at the same time if it is made correctly. If the engine is not to be visible, apart from the fan detail inside the air intake, it does not need painting with much detail. However, as I decided to open up an access panel, I painted the engine and spruced it up with some wiring detail. The top of the air intake that comes out of the upper fuselage has been scored to represent the mesh covering. (TO)

The compartment behind the engine is where the rear undercarriage is located, but this area in the Airfix kit is only represented by a plain box. Using plastic strip, fuse wire, some old resin pour lugs and plastic card, this area was detailed and after being painted Medium Sea Grey a watercolour wash was applied. To do this, watercolour paint is diluted down, applied by brush to the detailed parts, and then wiped away with a cloth, leaving some of the paint next to the raised detail, helping to dirty up the area and give it some depth. Above is a comparison of the compartment before and after detailing. (TO)

bay or cockpit. Although the techniques described seem pretty crude they do help to improve the detail of an otherwise quite plain seat.

With the cockpit assembled, a few scuffs of silver paint were added to represent chipped paintwork and the plain rear bulkhead had strips of plastic card, fuse wire and scrap plastic boxes added to represent the detail found on this section of the real aircraft. All of this detail was first painted using the same grey as the rest of the cockpit, then the boxes were painted black and the whole section were dry brushed using silver and white. The finished cockpit is then enclosed within the new Sea Harrier nose and the whole assembly, which is surprisingly heavy, was held together with tape whilst the glue dried.

The next assembly to tackle is the engine and in this model a quite well detailed Rolls Royce Pegasus is supplied. This is very easy to assemble, but unless an engine access panel is opened, or the wing taken off, none of this will be seen on the finished model. As I was opening up this area I decided that I would take the time to carefully paint the engine, including the ancillary bay mounted on the top of it, later adding fuse wire and scrap plastic to represent piping, wiring, boxes and framework.

Behind the engine is the rear undercarriage bay and in the Airfix kit this is just a plain box structure with no detail at all. I decided that I wanted to 'busy up' this area, but after drawing a blank with all of my reference material as to what the interior actually looked like I decided to use a little artistic licence. To form a solid forward wall, a piece of plastic card was placed over the cavity found here and plastic strip was used to represent stringers and formers on all surfaces. In amongst these were placed more little boxes, made from scrap plastic and old resin pour lugs with fuse wire being used to represent the wiring in between these boxes. The whole interior was painted Medium Sea Grey, with a darker grey being used for the wiring and the boxes were painted black. A liberal amount of the previously mentioned dry brushing and paint washing helps to dirty up this section which due to its proximity to the engine and any dirt blown up from the runway or jet blast, would be a quite grubby little cubby!

With the interior of the fuselage completed, both halves can now be joined, with more tape holding the parts together until the glue sets. Whilst the fuselage is drying the nose section can be attached and the previously built tailplane and fin can also be added. During the time that the fuselage, with its attached nose, is drying, the wings, which are very straightforward to build, can be assembled and left to one side.

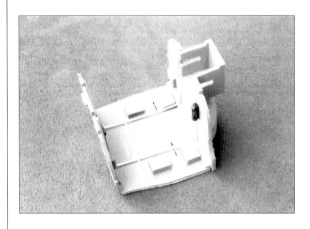

A view of the rear undercarriage bay, with just the plain plastic strip framework and a plastic card false wall in place, and the resin boxes and cylinder fitted. This is before the wiring was added and the main painting was done. (TO)

The finished rear undercarriage bay seen on the completed Sea Harrier FRS.1, showing just how effective the finished article looks. (TO)

Scratchbuilt air intake doors

All Harriers have small doors at the side of their main engine air intakes and these are auxiliary intakes that help more air to get to the engine when the aircraft is hovering or flying slowly. These doors are not powered at all; being sucked open by the engine when the suction of the engine is greater than the speed of the airflow that keeps them closed in forward flight. Consequently, when the aircraft is at rest gravity takes over and whilst the lower three doors drop down into the closed position, the upper four drop down open. The one remaining door in the middle normally remains closed, but on a windy day these, along with all the others if it is really windy, can open and close on their own, making a terrible noise.

In modelling terms this aspect of the Harrier family is largely ignored, with the doors normally being moulded tightly shut. Airfix are no different in this aspect, providing slight recesses on the side of the intakes where the doors are with no panel lines at all. The first thing to tackle is scribing in the locations of all of the doors. With the upper four doors the scribing is made deeper until they can be cut out. Depending on individual tastes these doors can either be retained or replaced with plastic card. I used plastic card for the 800 NAS model. Each of the intakes is an individual compartment and so each of the ones that have been opened needs to be separated from the others. To do this I cut thin strips of plastic card to shape and used these to provide a wall between each opened intake. The intakes also need a rear bulkhead to be made out of more plastic card and this was cut to size using the kit's air intake pieces as a template. When the internal air intake wall was added the outer part of it was painted black as it can be seen through the opened intake doors and also runs back into the engine bay.

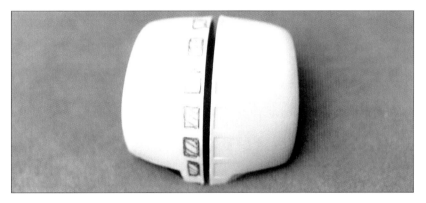

This view shows how the main engine air intakes look, before and after the auxiliary door detail was scribed on. The top is nearest to the camera: four of these doors need to be cut out and opened up. (TO)

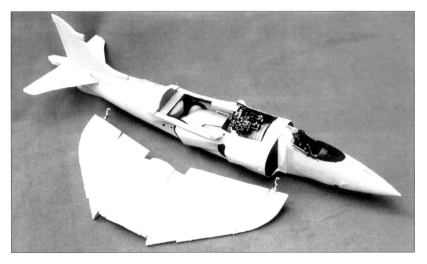

The parts are slowly coming together and looking like a Sea Harrier, with the nose and fuselage sections assembled and attached to each other, the tailplanes and fin added and the wings built up ready to be fitted. Just like the real aircraft the wing has to be lowered into place over the engine compartment. (TO)

The auxiliary intakes on any Harrier at rest really need to be opened up. They are there to provide the engine with more air when the aircraft is flying at slow speeds or hovering, and are sucked in by the suction of the engine: in normal powered flight they are forced shut by the airflow. When parked, gravity takes over, and while the lower doors are forced closed by gravity, the top four drop down into the open position. To replicate this the top four are opened up and tidied using a needle file. The original doors or plastic card replacements are then hung down and more plastic card is used to box off the side walls of each intake. This picture shows the front and rear of modified and unmodified parts, leaving off the rear wall for clarity. The plastic card sections on view represent the rear wall, a side wall and a replacement door. The tools required to carry this out are a knife, a needle file and a scriber. (TO)

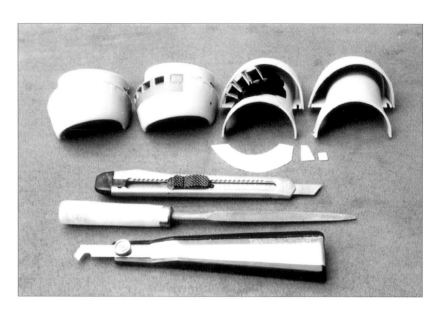

To save on all of this work however, a set of resin air intakes with the doors already moulded open are available from Heritage Aviation if this part of the construction does not suit.

Undercarriage

The undercarriage on the early Harriers and Sea Harrier is quite distinctive, comprising tandem nose and main wheels with smaller outrigger wheels at the wingtips. Airfix have provided for these quite well but they were designed to be able to move up and down, therefore they are a little bit crude. In the Sea Harrier release, new hubs are provided for the nose wheel and these are very nicely detailed but the rear wheel hubs are totally blank. Another throwback to the 1970s is the provision of rubber tyres for all of the wheels.

These tyres are very shiny and the first job with the undercarriage was to sand the tyres to remove the shine and make them more realistic. After this

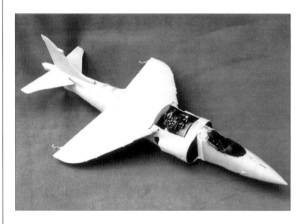

Now that the wings have been added to the fuselage the model looks like a Sea Harrier – but the wing still needs filler adding to it. Note how the outrigger undercarriage legs have been retracted to prevent them getting damaged during construction of the airframe. They are simply held in place with Blu-Tack for the time being. The nose will require a lot of filler to blend it with the fuselage. This has to be done before the air intakes can be fitted: it is also better to pre-paint this section before they are fitted, as access will be tricky later. (TO)

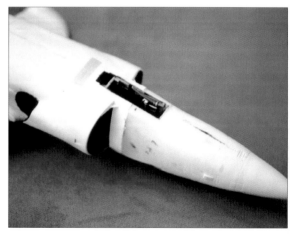

An underside view of the nose join, showing the step that was encountered at this position. This step can be reduced by either trimming off some of the outside of the interior wheel bay on the nose section or by filling and sanding. With this model a combination of both proved satisfactory in the end. (TO)

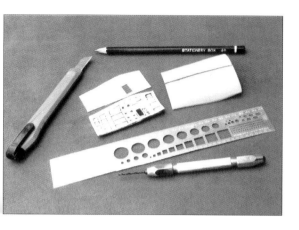

To make the interior detail for the opened-up engine ancillary bay doors, plastic card is cut into the same shape as the doors, using them as a template. The interior framework can then be drawn onto the plastic card using a pencil, and the insides cut out with a sharp knife. To make the holes, a pin vice is used to drill them out. When all of the cutting is completed, a framework resembling a brass etched fret is the result, and this is glued to the inside of the twin doors. After being painted white another watercolour wash is applied to give depth and realism to the part. This image shows the various stages of construction of this detail. (TO)

As the main parts of the Airfix kits are from the old Harrier GR.1 and GR.3 the air intakes have a wedge cut out at the top to allow the cockpit canopy to open. With the Sea Harrier however the canopy is raised above these intakes, so they need to be filled in. As they are quite deep, the best thing to use is Milliput two part filler that is best applied wet and can be smoothed into place with a wet finger. This view shows the white areas that have been filled, and the areas behind the recently fitted air intakes that have been filled using normal modelling filler. Both types of filler are illustrated. Also note the fire extinguisher holes in the wing roots, which have been drilled out. (TO)

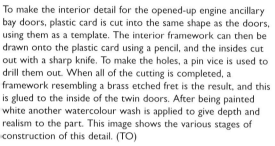

all of the plastic parts of the undercarriage, as well as the rubber hubs of the outrigger wheels, were painted Medium Sea Grey.

As mentioned the hubs of the rear main wheels were not very good, having no detail at all. To deal with this I cheated a bit and used a decal provided in the Harrier GR.3 kit, that replicates the holes in the hubs. Although not ideal, the resulting hubs do however look better, but for those who cannot live with rubber tyres or plain hubs, Heritage Aviation come to the rescue again as they provide a set of resin wheels with very nicely detailed hubs.

To finish off the undercarriage, the legs had brake lines added using more wire and once the decals from the kit were added along with a wash of more watercolour, they looked very nice indeed.

Main construction

With the model now taking shape and looking like a Sea Harrier it was time to start putting the final items together. At this stage it might be an idea to decide which parts are surplus to the model that you wish to build and take them out of the box. Otherwise, if this is not done there are parts and sprues taking up room in the box and it makes it hard to find the parts that you need. For the smaller parts that need to remain on an otherwise empty sprue, the main section of redundant sprue can be cut away, leaving a smaller section holding the parts. With this little tidy up done, construction can continue.

The first stage is to put the wings on. As with the real aircraft the wing centre section is also part of the upper fuselage and the whole wing is lowered down onto the fuselage. The fit is a little bit tight in places but a bit of prising gets it to fit quite well. There are also a few large gaps but these are easily covered in filler. Speaking of filler, whilst the tube is out the section on each side of the nose, where it joins with the fuselage is also a bit ragged and needs quite a bit of filler on each side to blend them in. These joints need to be filled in and sanded before the air intakes can be fitted so now is a good time to do it. From here construction whizzes along, with the windscreen and undercarriage being fitted and most of the filling and sanding can be completed.

As the engine ancillary bay was to be opened up on one side, the two doors on the left-hand side, which is the side to be opened, need to be cut off. This is a simple matter of cutting along the moulded line along the centre of the part that covers this section, but don't fall into the trap that I nearly fell into. At the front corner of each front door on each side there is a triangular part that is supposed to stay attached to the fuselage. I only realized this later on during construction, whilst looking at a picture and wondering why my doors did not look like theirs! The triangular section needs to be cut off the door soon and attached to the fuselage.

To detail the inside face of the ancillary bay doors a piece of plastic card was used with the actual door piece serving as a template and cut to the same shape. The internal rib detail was then drawn onto the plastic card and the sections in between were cut out using a sharp craft knife, with the small round holes being drilled out using a pin vice. When this was finished the resulting piece is something similar to a brass etched fret and can be simply glued onto the interior of the door, painted white and later on given a 'wash' of black watercolours. This piece was then left aside until later.

The next big construction job is to add the air intakes. These intakes are not the best fit in the world, but after a bit of fiddling, they were attached, making sure that the internal intake wall meets with the front of the engine and the sides of the forward fuselage. As I mentioned the fit of these parts are not ideal and a lot of filler is required to blend the outside of the intakes in with the rest of the fuselage.

A point not mentioned in the instructions is that whilst the Harrier GR.1 and 2 had a cut out in the top of the air intakes for the canopy to slide open, the Sea Harrier does not have this cut out, due to the canopy being much higher. As the kit, just like the Sea Harrier itself, is derived from the earlier Harriers, this cut out needs to be filled. As it is quite deep, usual model filler will not be very successful, so I used Milliput. This filler comes in two different varieties, normal and fine. Both comprise two separate rolls of putty that when mixed together form a very good waterproof filler. I find that this filler is better used when wet and I used the fine variety to fill up the gap, smoothing it into place with a wet finger. The engine ancillary bay door that was to remain closed was added at this stage also, along with the triangular piece that was removed from the front door on the other side.

Painting

Some sections of the model require pre painting due to the fact that after construction they are impossible to get to otherwise. These areas are the fuselage above the nozzle area, which needs painting before adding the wings and the side of the new nose that ends up being inside the air intakes once these pieces are fixed in place.

A close-up of the engine ancillary bay double doors, with the triangular piece that stays on the fuselage cut off, along with the internal framework that arches over the engine bay, and the pin vice used to drill the holes in this piece. (TO)

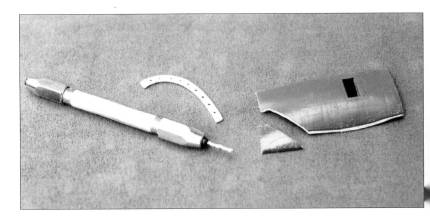

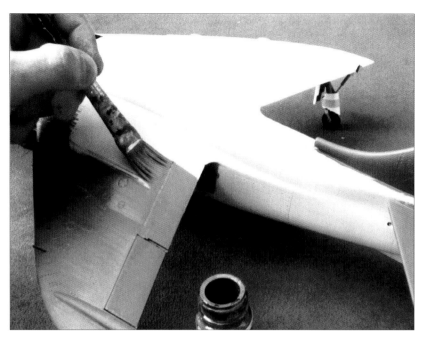

When hand painting a large model such as this, it is best to use a large brush. For flat areas the best coverage is given using a flat brush: I used one for the wings and tail. A rounder brush was used in more contoured areas such as the nose, fuselage and fuel tanks. When hand-painting, always try to paint in the direction of the airflow. For the grey and white scheme I used two coats of Acrylic grey followed by two further coats of Xtracolor Extra Dark Sea Grey applied with a brush for the upper surfaces, and four coats of white applied from a spray can for the underneath, with brushed-on satin Coal Black for the nose cone. The spray has to be applied before any enamel paint: if the spray, whilst wet, comes into contact with them, the enamels will crinkle up. To touch up the white paintwork Humbrol gloss white enamel was used. (TO)

An acrylic undercoat for the upper grey colour was used, the same colour as used for the cockpit interior, Extra Dark Sea Grey from Polyscale. This colour was too light a shade to use for the final coat, but due to the way that these acrylics go on very smoothly by brush it would serve as an excellent undercoat.

I know that most serious modellers use an airbrush nowadays, but I have neither the facilities nor the inclination to use one of these. I find hand brushing very enjoyable and seem to be able to get a decent finish, using the right brushes for the right jobs, although I do sometimes cheat by using spray cans for colours that are hard to hand brush well. One such colour which is hard to hand brush over a large area is white and as this model was certainly large I used a can of Halfords Appliance White for the under surfaces.

A view of the canopy whilst being masked up for the Light Sea Grey coloured canopy sealant, and the finished item ready to be attached to the model. Note how the MDC chord has been painted inside the roof of the canopy and that the rear bulkhead has received a watercolour wash to enhance the detail. (TO)

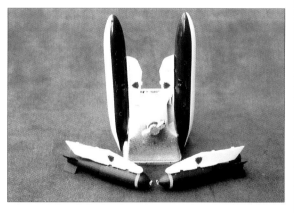

The finished underwing armament for the 800 NAS model, with the decals in place. The underwing drop tanks have been assembled and sanded, with the raised panel line replaced by engraving. This was done by running a scriber along the side of the raised detail and then sanding the raised detail off. The vice shown was used to hold the tanks while they were painted in the same colours as the aircraft: the bombs were painted Dark Green with Bronze Green tails, with decals for the yellow bands.

The ADEN cannons: a finished version for the grey and white Sea Harrier FRS.1 is shown next to an unpainted set. (TO)

For a model the size of the Sea Harrier, a large brush is a must, to be able to cover the area and I used two of these. A flat brush is used to cover the flat areas such as the wings and a rounder brush is used for the difficult contours such as the area around the nozzle pipes.

After a few light coats of spray the white undersides are soon completed and dry very quickly, thanks to the type of hard wearing acrylic paint used. The white areas were then masked off with Tamiya tape and a few light coats of acrylic grey were brushed on to serve as the undercoat for the final upper surface colour. This final colour was Extra Dark Sea Grey by Xtracolor and it is a gloss enamel paint. I find this to be the best representation of this colour, but it is quite hard to hand brush onto a model, hence the acrylic undercoat first.

Using the brushes described earlier a thin coat of paint was applied and then left to dry overnight. This initial coat was quite streaky, as usual with this paint, but when another coat was added next day the result was a very nice even gloss finish. When the masking tape was removed the usual overspill was tidied up using scrapers, sanding blocks, Humbrol Gloss White enamel and more Xtracolor grey. To finish off the painting the nose cone was marked out using pictures as a guide and was painted using Humbrol Satin Coal Black enamel. Other items such as the under wing pylons, fuel tanks and bombs were also painted.

Decals

I used the decals from the Airfix kit. Some of the images were a little blurred but by using the best parts from a few sheets, decent examples were found.

One of the great things about using Xtracolor paints is that they dry gloss, so they are ready for decals to be applied, without having to paint on a coat of

The finished engine ancillary bay showing the extra detail added here and the triangular section attached to the fuselage at the forward corner. (TO)

gloss varnish first. The actual decal sheet is the same size as the box and it is 'really huge'. It has options for three Royal Navy grey and white schemed aircraft, one in the low viz Falklands scheme, another in overall Dark Sea Grey and an Indian Navy aircraft in dark grey and pale grey. All of the schemes are striking but for this project I chose the grey and white Sea Harrier of 800 NAS, being the first scheme worn by the FRS.1.

I always like to find out a little about the aircraft that I am building and I will give a brief history at this point. XZ454 of 800 Naval Air Squadron (NAS) dates back to 1980. This aircraft was one of the first batch of Sea Harriers to be delivered and on 20 May 1980 it was the first one ever to land on HMS *Invincible*. Unfortunately at the end of 1980, after less than a year in service, flown by Lt. Cmdr. Mike Blisset, it was also the first Sea Harrier to be lost, when it struck the mast or ski jump of the *Invincible* during a fast fly by and crashed. Luckily the pilot ejected and survived with minor injuries.

A close-up of the finished nose wheel, showing the extra brake piping added around the leg, the effective use of decals, and the excellent detail of the kit wheel hubs that has been highlighted by the use of a watercolour wash. (TO)

Back to the model. When applying the decals to the model, it is better to cut off a few decals at a time from the sheet and put them onto the model. I find that if too many decals are left lying around in water for a long time they can become damaged and if the decal numbers float away it is be hard to identify some of the smaller stencils. I found that all of the decals went on very well and they were easily sealed in place with a couple of coats of gloss varnish.

Finishing touches

With the models now painted and the decals in place it is now just a matter of adding the fiddly bits. The first of these are the ADEN cannon pods, of which two are carried under the fuselage, and of course these should have already been pre-painted. Next onto the pylons, fuel tanks, armament, canopy, opened up engine bay door and antennas.

As all of the pylons, tanks and armament have also been pre-painted, with the decals applied it is simply a case of attaching them, making sure that the correct pylons go in place under the wings with each one mounted at a slope in relation to the angle of the wing. This aircraft is shown in the role of a fighter-bomber, carrying two 1,000lb bombs.

Next, the canopy: after attaching the plastic slide rails and blending them in with filler, the framework was painted in the same colour as the interior. Next the Xtracolor external colour was painted on. When this was dry the canopy was masked up and Light Aircraft Grey was painted on to represent the sealant strip around the edges of the framework and the rescue arrow decals were added. To paint the MDC chord, which on the real aircraft detonates to allow the seat to pass through the canopy when the pilot is ejecting, it is a simple matter of roughly painting it using Acrylic Medium Sea Grey. Before it starts to dry, wipe off any excess with a damp cloth and what remains in the internal recess are nice crisply painted lines. I must mention that I nearly had a disaster with the canopy when a drop of superglue dripped onto it. After a few choice words I scraped off the glue with a knife, polished it with toothpaste to remove the marks, which got it back to being smooth and another quick polish with a clean cloth restored the clarity.

Before the opened up engine bay door can be mounted in position an internal section of framework has to be constructed onto which are mounted the rods that support the opened doors. This framework follows the contours of the inside of the doors themselves and it is these that are used as a template to form the outer surface of a section of framework that was cut from thick plastic card. After this frame section has been cut out and dry fitted to make sure it fits in place, small holes are drilled into it using a pin vice. The section is then painted white,

The completed 1981 Sea Harrier FRS.1 of 800 NAS, with opened engine ancillary bay, and carrying two 1,000lb bombs. (TO)

attached to the inside of the engine bay where it arches over the ancillary parts and the supporting rods are superglued into place to hold open the engine bay doors, in the same manner as a car bonnet. Last of all the various antennas are glued into place and painted.

ABOVE Another 1/24 Sea Harrier, but this time the latest FA2 version which has been built using the Airfix Harrier GR.3 kit with the addition of the hefty resin conversion set from Heritage Aviation. This model was built before the advent of the new Airfix FRS.1 kit, requiring the whole nose to be replaced and due to the amount of resin involved it results in a very heavy end that requires a strong shelf to support the weight. It is painted in the current overall Medium Sea Grey colour scheme that seems to apply to all front line Fleet Air Arm aircraft, and wears the newly introduced full colour squadron markings of 800 NAS to help brighten it up. (TO)

LEFT The underside of the FA2 showing its two ADEN cannon pods, two Sidewinder missiles and 100-gallon underwing fuel tanks. The Royal Navy Sea Harriers regularly carry their cannon pods and are the only British Harriers able to use a cannon armament. The RAF GR.7s still carry cannon pods but these are usually unarmed as they are still not cleared to fire their cannons, with one of the redundant empty pods reportedly used for carrying ECM equipment instead.

ABOVE The newly-introduced colourful squadron markings of 800 NAS. The squadron markings are not available in decal form in any scale unfortunately, and were hand painted onto the model.

LEFT A close up of the highly detailed resin seat with seat straps that are moulded in and realistically painted, as well as the resin engine air intakes showing the blow-in doors in the open position. Also shown is the bolt-on refuelling probe and the wind vane in front of the cockpit, which shows the direction of the wind when the aircraft is in the hover.

Making a display base

Building a display base for a 1/24-scale model may be a bit unrealistic, but in 1/72 and 1/48 it's a popular option, and one worth doing. Many though are daunted by the prospect of trying to produce a realistic and detailed base on which to mount models, but there are options. You can opt to buy one ready made, or you can create one from scratch with little expense. In this section we'll take a step-by-step look at how to create a really good base, with authentic details such as cracks, oil and fuel stains, concrete panelling, and grass verges.

RIGHT This photograph of a Harrier GR.3 at RAF Mildenhall in May 1985 is interesting for the hard-standing, mainly because it is so clean and featureless. This part of the taxi way is not normally used to park aircraft and so all the oil spills and general wear and tear are 'missing'. This would be a little dull and plain if replicated exactly as seen here. (GC)

RIGHT A little more interesting this time for the Harrier modeller. Note the large blocks of concrete that make up the hard-standing. Dark grey tar is used to fill the gaps between these and the inevitable cracks that are apparent all around the blocks. (GC)

This picture of the GR.3 at rest is very interesting because it illustrates the great variety of surface texture and appearance – air shows are good because you can get access to parts of the base like this not normally possible. Here the newer, light concrete taxi way is visible in the background. In the foreground the much darker, more heavily worn concrete can be seen. Note too the tyre marks left by vehicles. The yellow line indicates the track pilots should take to and from the runway. All these features are excellent options to incorporate into your base – helping to show off your Harrier scale model. (GC)

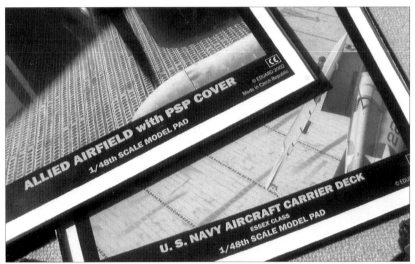

One option for you to consider early on is whether to use one of Eduard's excellent pre-formed plastic bases. These terrific bases authentically represent specific surfaces such as carrier deck planking and metal PSP plating. To be honest the pattern and design is more appropriate for World War II subjects, but with a little work they could easily be adapted for use with your Harrier models. All that is needed is to paint them up: the cover illustrations that come with the products are a good guide for the finish you need. (GC)

The availability of MDF board provides a great opportunity for modellers to create an ideal base for displaying their models. Most of the boards I use are purchased from model shows, where someone has already gone to the trouble of routing the edges and cutting the board into useful shapes and sizes. They are invariably inexpensive. If you are going to cut this type of material be sure to wear an appropriate dust/particle mask, as the dusk can be toxic if inhaled. (GC)

TOP Armed with your base it's time to select the paints you'll need. I have included the ones that I use on just about all my 'concrete' bases. Polyscale acrylic paints (available from Hannants) are excellent for this. Here you can see Old Concrete and Dirt and Mud. The Old Concrete is simply sprayed or brushed onto your MDF board. Because it is acrylic, it dries very quickly. The Mud and Dirt are used to weather the edges of the grassed area you can see in the accompanying photos: it is added with a broad brush and dabbed into areas of grass that have become worn. The Tamiya Smoke is good for accentuating and creating shadow along the edges of the concrete blocks. (GC)

MIDDLE I think that grassed areas provide good contrast and variety to the base. The material you see here is available from good model shops everywhere and railway model shops seem to have the best range. The grass comes in small rolls in various colours to simulate the real thing. It can look especially realistic when weathered and dirtied up with Mud and Dirt paints. Simply cut out the shape you want with a pair of scissors and glue it down with PVA glue. I use Evostick white wood glue. A useful tip is to put an old book or flat weight over the grass while it dries to avoid bubbling; and be sure to work quickly with the PVA, covering every tiny area of the paper backing paper, as this will also help to avoid bubbling of the surface. (GC)

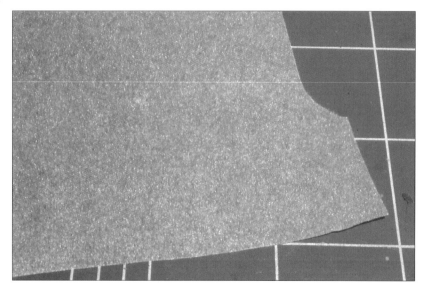

BOTTOM The next stage is to mark out the concrete blocks using a graphite pencil and ruler. In quarter scale I mark out squares about 3 inches across, and this looks about the right scale to me. When this is done and you have a checkerboard effect, I rub a finger along the lines to blur them slightly. They are then over sprayed with Tamiya Smoke (X-19). This versatile paint gives you a nice ghosting of the lines and helps create a 3D effect. Focus a little more spray around the joins at the corners of each block. Your spray pressure should be turned down to about 10 psi for this so as to help control and accuracy. (GC)

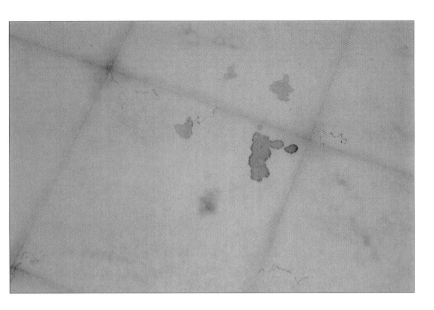

Hard-standing areas where aircraft are parked invariably have plenty of oil stains and drops on the concrete. These are easily simulated using Tamiya Smoke dripped onto the surface with a cocktail stick. A wide variety of stain sizes can be achieved with this method but be careful not to overdo the effect. Note also in this picture and others the small cracks in the concrete, achieved by simply adding pencil cracks where appropriate. These seem to congregate around the corners and edges of the blocks. (GC)

It can be useful to weather the grassed areas further by adding Dirt and Mud paint, or even real earth as seen here. It adheres to PVA very well and helps the grassed areas look realistically worn – especially good if you are trying to represent summer or drier climates.

The base is nearly finished now and all that's left is to paint the edges matt black. I use a broad brush for this and hand-paint it, but you could just as easily mask off the surface and spray the black from your airbrush or a can.

There is no doubt that displaying your models on a realistic base can give a lot of pleasure to all who look at them. The possibilities for Harrier scale modellers are even more varied, with forest clearings and carrier deck-standings all good candidates for creativity. (GC)

Kits and accessories available

Since 1962 we have seen kits produced that have followed the development of the Harrier in its different forms right through to the latest variants. Mainly produced in mainstream injection moulded form, we have also seen some gaps filled with resin kits. As well as the kits, a plethora of decals and accessories have been produced to enhance the subject for the modeller, so much so that it would not be possible to list all of them here. The list below breaks down the kits into the differing scales, with the caveat that there will be a few gaps, with kits deleted or newer kits being produced. Also, note that a number of kits, particularly the ex-Frog/Novo Harrier GR.1, have been released under several labels at the same time.

1/144 scale
Academy
Sea Harrier FRS.1: typical of kits in this small scale, details are limited but construction fairly simple.

This is the ESCI MDD AV-8A 'Matador': the box art shows a US Marines Corps AV-8A in full colour markings with a Spanish aircraft behind it.

The ESCI AV-8A US Marines Corps Harrier, in 1/72.

Dragon

AV-8B Harrier II: part of a range of modern combat aircraft produced by Dragon, the AV-8B is another small, simplified kit of this aircraft that features minimal detail.

Revell

Revell also produce an AV-8B Harrier II in this scale.

1/72 scale
Airfix

P.1127: recently re-issued and featured in this book. The oldest Harrier family kit there is, but one that can be improved and reworked into a decent replica. Cockpit detail minimal, the surface requires attention.

Harrier GR.1: the original production version of the Harrier from 1969 that was a typical kit of its day, cockpit rather sparse but otherwise not bad at the time.

Harrier GR.3: updated from the GR.1 this kit still remains in the lists today. It was updated at the same time as the full-size aircraft.

Harrier GR.5/7: the introduction of the AV-8B/GR.5 series of aircraft saw Airfix produce new kits also. Accurate in shape but requiring a little attention by addition of cockpit detail. Both versions have been boxed as separate kits.

Harrier T.10/AV-8B: a new version of the trainer, which has been released in both boxings by Airfix. Apart from the differing fuselage the kits are to the same level of detail as the GR.5/7 kits with further work required on the cockpits.

ESCI

Harrier GR.1, GR.3, Sea Harrier FRS.1, AV-8A: currently out of production, but at the time of writing Italeri were about to re-release the Sear Harrier FRS.1. These kits date from the early 1980s and are among the best Harrier kits produced. At the time when kit manufacturers were looking to make ultimate use of every mould these kits had common main parts with differing parts for each version. Cockpit detail was good if not stunning and the overall level of detail and accuracy made these popular kits with the modeller. Still much sought after.

Frog/Novo

Harrier GR.1: You may wonder why I listed this when Frog was sold in 1976. Well, the same kit still turns up in several East European ranges. Very much to the level of detail as the Airfix GR.1 this kit was not bad in its day but is rather dated currently. Having said that, with a little work a reasonable replica can be produced.

Fujimi

Harrier GR.1/AV-8A, GR.3, Sea Harrier FRS.1: released around the same time as the ESCI kits these were sold as the best kits around. Nicely broken down with good detail, they suffered from very poor fit of the parts needing a good deal of filler and effort by the modeller. Not currently in the list but possibly kits that may return, one day.

Hasegawa

Hasegawa currently produce the followingkits: GR.1, GR.3, AV-8B, AV-8B Desert Harrier, AV-8B+, GR.5, GR.7, and the FRS.1 Sea Harrier. At the time of writing, they announced a forthcoming range of 1/48-scale Harrier IIs.

The ESCI 1/72 Laser Harrier GR.3, amongst the best kits of the Harrier family. (TO)

Two of the latest versions of the Harrier II to be released by Hasegawa in 1/72 – the AV-8B Desert Harrier in Desert Storm two-tone grey camouflage with shark's teeth, and the AV-8B+ with the radar nose, in the latest F-16 type scheme. (TO)

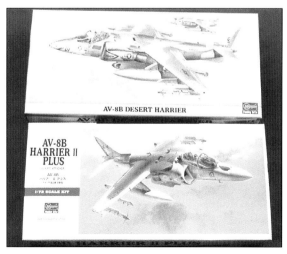

TOP The 1/72 Hasegawa Sea Harrier FRS.1. (TO)

ABOVE The 1/72 Hasegawa Harrier GR.3 with superb box art to boot. This is arguably the best kit available of the Harrier GR.3 in 1/72, just pipping the ESCI kit. (TO)

Heritage Aviation

P.1127/Kestrel: this UK-based resin manufacturer has produced accurate resin kits of both subjects. The P.1127 was popular when the Airfix kit was dropped but both kits feature the differences between the two aircraft and have nicely engraved details and good interiors. As well as producing the variants that were actually built, Heritage have covered the proposed versions such as the T.1127 trainer and the twin fuselage Tuning Fork version.

Harrier T.2/4: with the loss of the rather nice Humbrol Bobcat kit the only option for building the trainer version of the Harrier is the excellent little T.2/4 kit from Heritage produced in fine cast resin with metal details.

Humbrol Bobcat

Harrier T.4: now rather hard to find, this is a simplified but accurate kit of the RAF trainer version. These kits had almost snap-together construction methods but were accurate and covered unusual subjects. Sadly for some reasons the kits never made their way into the Airfix or Heller ranges – perhaps one day they will?

Italeri

AV-8B Harrier II/GR.7: typical of the kits produced by this Italian manufacturer with good if somewhat simplified detail in the cockpit. They also produce a TAV-8B two-seater trainer kit.

Matchbox

Sea Harrier FRS.1: the first Sea Harrier kit to hits the streets, timed just right for the Falklands War in 1982. It sold superbly at first but was not one of the better kits from this manufacturer. Lacking in detail, it was more like a beginner's kit than a serious subject for the dedicated modeller. Matchbox have also produced the Harrier GR.3 and GR.1.

The Revell Harrier GR.7. This is the Hasegawa kit but in a Revell box. (TO)

1/48 ⊙ ROYAL NAVY SEA HARRIER FRS.1   TAMIYA

Tamiya's 1/48-scale Royal Navy Sea Harrier FRS.1. (TO)

Revell
Harrier GR.7: as part of Revell's on-going plans to rebox other kits, they have released the Hasegawa AV-8B as the RAF GR.7 version with different decals. The comments regarding the kits are the same as for the Hasegawa kit.

1/48 scale
Airfix
Harrier GR.3, Sea Harrier FRS.1, Sea Harrier F/A.2: the GR.3 is featured here in the book but the same basic kit with sutble changes has been the basis for all of the Airfix Harrier kits. Cockpit detail needs a little extra work and some other details such as grilles/intakes are rather basic, but it is sound in shape. If you want to build a trainer then check out Heritage Aviations T.2/4 trainer conversion.

Monogram
AV-8B: although now seemingly an old kit this actually makes up into a rather nice replica. A bit of a personal favourite, the kit assembles fairly easily and has excellent levels of detail.

Tamiya
Harrier GR.1, Sea Harrier FRS.1: dating from over 20 years ago these kits are still excellent. Usually on the current Tamiya lists, the GR.1 was later modified to allow the release of the FRS.1. Good levels of detail throughout.

1/32 scale
Revell
Harrier GR.1: a rare beast! Not seen in kit shops for some years, but can still be picked up from second hand dealers, this is the only 1/32-scale Harrier kit. Typical of the Revell kits of the period with raised details, gimmicks galore and rather simple detailing for a kit of this size. But if you want a Harrier in this scale, it's the only game in town.

Trumpeter
Announced at the time of writing, this Chinese manufacturer is to release a 1/32 AV-8B kit.

1/24 scale
Airfix
Harrier GR.1, GR.3 Sea Harrier FRS.1: the biggies! For a long time the GR.1 was the only version available until the last few years when Airfix saw fit to update

the kit. First to come was the GR.3 with suitable new parts, followed recently by the Sea Harrier FRS.1. This too has a multitude of new parts.

Decals and other accessories

In recent years a steadily growing number of small companies have begun to produce conversion and detail sets, as well as alternative decals, for various Harrier kits.

Decals

The growth of new decals companies has been very rapid. To list every sheet by every company would be pointless, as the market is so fluid that sheets come and go on a regular basis, but it is interesting to take a look at the history of Harrier decals.

When aftermarket decals began to appear, one British company had an unchallenged name when it came to detail and quality: Modeldecal. The brainchild of Mike Silk and Dick Ward, best known for his artwork for Airfix, produced a range of highly detailed sheets that were extremely popular with modellers. Modeldecal led the way in terms of just how much information could be crammed onto the sheets and their instructions, without having really been bettered yet.

In the USA, the main producer were Microscale, aka Superscale, who were very prolific. Although the decals themselves were very good, the instruction sheets often left the modeller having to check his references for more information. Indeed sometimes an entirely different variant was shown on the instructions compared to the decals' intended model.

Gradually more companies, such as Two Bobs, Aviation Workshop, SKY Models, Modeldecal and Fineline, have produced decals for Harriers of many types, serving with various air forces, and in several scales (but mostly 1/72 and 1/48).

Conversion/detail sets

The range of detail sets is ever-changing with new companies being introduced to the modelling fraternity on a regular basis.

In 1/72 scale, replacement intakes with dropped doors are available from Heritage Aviation, which gets round the problem encountered on most Harrier kits. These have also been produced in 1/48 and 1/24 scales for the larger kits. With Heritage intakes there is a casting mount that needs to be sanded off but take care doing this or you'll have to apply filler, making yourself more work.

Heritage have also produced detail sets for the 1/48-scale Airfix kits that give more detail in the cockpits. These resin sets once cleaned up and painted can look very convincing. For the 1/24-scale kits, there are cockpit sets and weighted wheels.

Heritage Aviation's T.1127 resin kit. (GA)

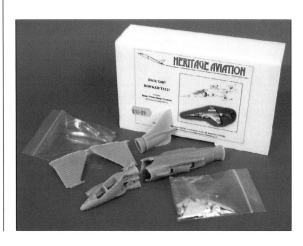

With regard to etched brass, ED Models in Birmingham, UK, have produced a growing range of detail sets for a number of years, usually for cockpit interiors. When using etched brass, ensure you prime it before painting and wash it before use, to remove any flux from the surfaces. As well as the etched brass sets, ED Models used to produce C-scale conversion sets, many of which have been taken up by Airwaves. These included a Harrier T.2 conversion for use with the Bobcat kit.

For the Sea Harrier modeller, the introduction of the FA.2 into Fleet Air Arm service was met with the release of a suitable conversion from Maintrack Models, but this has now been deleted. It may be available as a second hand item but with the planned release of the Aviation Workshop kit this may become a surplus item.

LEFT Modeldecal sheet No.74, for 1/72 scale: all Modeldecals sheets are in this scale. This sheet features decals for the Harrier GR.3, T.2A and the T.4. It also contains decals for NATO F-16s. (TO)

BELOW LEFT SKY Models decal sheet 48-028 in 1/48 scale. (TO)

BOTTOM LEFT Modeldecal sheet 67, featuring Sea Harriers from the Falklands era, plus decals for Tornados and Puma helicopters.

BELOW RIGHT Fineline sheet 2005a features the anniversary Sea Harrier decals used by 899 NAS. (TO)

BOTTOM RIGHT Modeldecal sheet 75, featuring a Harrier T4N. (TO)

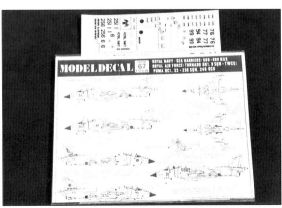

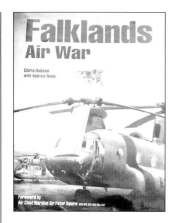

Further reading and research

As with almost any type of aircraft, there is a wide selection of further reading material available, much of which is useful to the modeller. As you would expect it is difficult to list everything in print, so I have chosen to pick out a number of books that will provide good reference. Regarding magazine articles, it would take up a large chunk of this book simply to list all of them so beyond a few particularly good examples, I have opted to list the major magazine titles that have featured the Harrier on numerous occasions.

Books

Harrier & Sea Harrier by Roy Braybrook, published by Osprey. In-depth history of the Harrier from day one to the late 1980s.

Harrier – The Vertical Reality by Roy Braybrook, published by The Royal Benevolent Fund Enterprises (1996). A first-class publication with quality photographs throughout. The early Hawker P.1127/Kestrel is covered well here as are the later variants and the air arms that use the Harrier.

Harrier – Inside and Out by Mark Attrill, published by The Crowood Press (2002). An absolute must for the Harrier modeller. This stunnig book has all the colour photographs you could wish for – both inside and out, as the title suggests. Especially good for the later RAF and RN Harriers.

Harrier in Action by Don Linn, published by Squadron/Signal. Now nearly 20 years old this title is crammed full of useful photographs. There is strong coverage of USMC AV-8s too.

Harrier (Combat Legends series) by Glenn Ashley, published by Airlife. Up-to-date history of the Harrier in its many forms.

Harrier (Modern Combat Aircraft No.4), published by Ian Allan. Another fully-detailed history of the aircraft dating back to the mid-1980s.

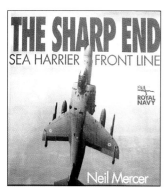

Harrier (Warbirds Illustrated No.20), by Michael Gethring, published by Arms and Armour. Photo history of the Harrier from the P.1127 through to the Falklands War.

Harrier – Super Profile by Chris Chant, published by Winchmore Publishing Services (1983). A first-class publication with quality photographs throughout. The early Hawker P.1127/Kestrel is covered well here as are the later variants and the air arms that use the Harrier.

Harrier – The VSTOL Warrior by John Dibbs and Tony Holmes, published by Osprey Publishing Ltd.

Harrier at War by Alfred Price, published by Ian Allan.

Sea Harrier over the Falklands by Lt.Cmdr. Sharky Ward DSC AFC RN, published by Leo Cooper.

No Escape Zone by Lt. Nick Richardson, published by Little Brown & Co.

The Sharp End: Sea Harrier Front Line by Neil Mercer, published by Airlife.

Falklands Air War by Chris Hobson with Andew Noble, published by Midland Counties.

BAe/McDonnell Douglas Harrier by Andy Evans, published by Crowood.

Fleet Air Arm by Neil Mercer, published by Airlife.

Royal Navy Aircraft since 1945 by Ray Williams, published by Naval Institute Press.

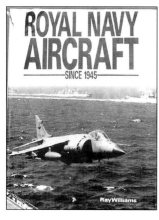

Yeovilton (Superbase series No.22) by Mike Verier, published by Osprey Publishing Ltd. This title is no longer available from the publishers, but libraries or specialist second-hand bookshops may still be able to find you a copy. Good reference for base scenarios.

Magazines

Scale Aircraft Modelling. An excellent monthly magazine crammed full of a great deal on the Harrier over the years with good coverage of camouflage and markings. Vol.23 No.11 (January 2002) contains features on the BAe Harrier GR.5, GR.7 and T.10

Scale Aviation Modeller International. Another good title that has featured the Harrier, perhaps to a lesser degree than *Scale Aircraft Modelling* though.

Scale Models. The original publication before its re-birth featured Harrier material shortly after the Falklands War. Old copies can be picked up from specialist magazine and book dealers.

Finescale Modeler. This American modelling magazine has featured the occasional article that is of use to the Harrier modeller.

Aeroplane Magazine. The November 2002 issue contains an article entitled 'Birth of the Harrier: The Hawker P.1127 & Kestrel.'

World Airpower Journal. The following issues contain detailed articles on the Harrier: Vol.6, summer 1991; Vol.32, spring 1998; Vol.41, summer 2000.

Websites

There are dozens of dedicated sites that feature the Harrier and every modeller will have his own favourite. By entering a search for such subjects as Harrier, BAe, McDonnell Douglas, Rolls Royce, RAF, Royal Navy, USMC, Spanish Navy, Thai Navy, Italian Navy, Indian Navy and so on, you will find exactly what you seek. One particularly impressive site is *www.harrier.org.uk*.

If I were to suggest one website that you really should visit then it is the one run by Nick Greenall of IPMS(UK)'s Harrier Special Interest Group (or SIG). This excellent site can be found at *http://harrier.hyperlinx.cz*. You can e-mail Nick at *nickgreenall@jngreenall.freeserve.co.uk*.

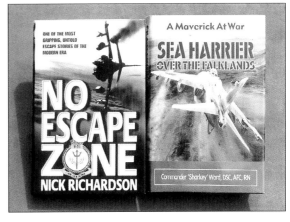

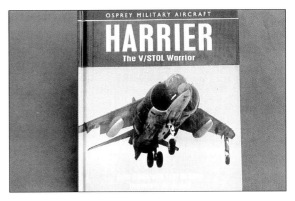

Museums, collections and reference

With the Harrier still being a vital part of the various military air arms it serves with, very few are located in museums. The RAF Museum at Hendon, UK, has a Harrier GR.3 on display, and the Science Museum in London has a P.1127 (XP831). A few other Harriers have joined museums around the UK. At Duxford there is XZ133; at the Museum of Flight at East Fortune, there is a GR.3, XV277; and another GR.3 (XV748) is on display at the Yorkshire Air Museum at Elvington.

The only Sea Harrier currently on display in the UK is XZ493, located in the Fleet Air Arm Museum at Yeovilton, Somerset. This exhibit is actually the main fuselage and wings of a Harrier GR.3 with the nose of XZ493 added. This nose was part of the wreckage of the aircraft recovered from the bottom of the Adriatic after it crashed in the 1990s during operations over Bosnia. As the upgraded FA2s are being withdrawn from service, they are being allocated to museums, with one already being allocated to Yeovilton.

In the US one of the XV-6 Kestrels is preserved at the USAF Museum at Dayton but it is unlikely any AV-8A/Bs are on show.

The best chance to see the Harrier up close and personal is at an air show. Throughout Europe and the US, British and American Harriers of varying marks are always popular participants, thrilling crowds wherever they appear. If you happen to live in an area of the world where no Harriers are operated, your only hope may well be books or magazines. To help out, here are some super images of 'the real deal' up close.

A Harrier GR.7 of 20(R) Squadron, RAF, in the current two-tone grey scheme, taken at Waddington, 1999. (TO)

ABOVE An RAF Harrier GR.7. This picture, and the others that follow, were taken during the RIAT2000 airshow at Cottesmore.

This GR.7 'ZG501/72' is in the charge of No.3 Squadron at RAF Cottesmore. (PDS)

Close-up of the nose cone showing the red cup over the ARBS sensor and FLIR probe over the nose. The creamy tip antennas are part of the ECM Zeus system. (PDS)

ABOVE A close-up of the extended in-flight refueling probe and lowered auxiliary upper intake doors due to the effect of gravity. (PDS)

BELOW A close-up of RAF No.3 Squadron's markings on GR.7 ZG501/72 and the standard blue/red roundel. (PDS)

ABOVE Close-up of wing pylons and the outrigger wheel on GR.7 ZG501/72. (PDS)

BELOW Close-up of TIALD pod under GR.7 ZG501/72's belly fitted on a dedicated pylon. Note also the front retractable LID surface. (PDS)

ABOVE Close-up of the rear nozzle and the exhaust heat shield plate on GR.7 ZG501/72. Note also the empty gun pod fitted. (PDS)

RIGHT Close-up of GR.7 ZD410/39's tail and the inclined tail surfaces. Note No.3 Squadron's colours on the fin tip. (PDS)

Close-up of GR.7 ZG501/72's front undercarriage with white leg and black hydraulic cables. (PDS)

Close-up of GR.7 ZG501/72's main undercarriage with white leg and double wheel track. (PDS)

The cockpit of a full size AV-8B/Harrier II. Obviously much cleaner than operational
aircraft this mock up shows the colours and location of all relevant details in the
newer generation of Harrier aircraft. (BAe)

ABOVE A Harrier GR.7 of No.4 Squadron, RAF, Waddington, 1999. (TO)

BELOW A Harrier GR.7 of 20(R) Squadron, RAF, in special airshow livery, arriving at the Malta Airshow; Luqa, Malta, 2001. (TO)

Index

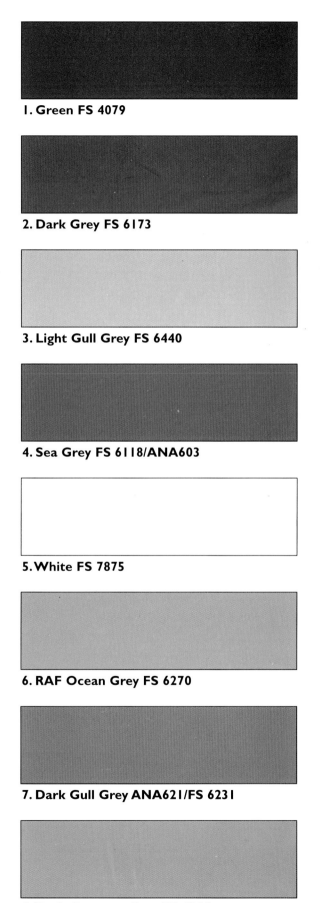

1. Green FS 4079

2. Dark Grey FS 6173

3. Light Gull Grey FS 6440

4. Sea Grey FS 6118/ANA603

5. White FS 7875

6. RAF Ocean Grey FS 6270

7. Dark Gull Grey ANA621/FS 6231

8. Dark Compass Grey FS 6320

1. Green FS 4079

The standard RAF Green used since the end of World War II. Notice on full-size aircraft how the paint tends to fade slightly and where touched up is much darker, particularly on aircraft operating in climates with much stronger sun, such as Harriers used in Belize. If you slightly lighten the paint, when you add a wash the colour will darken. US equivalent was used on the AV-8A.

2. Dark Grey FS 6173

Used in conjunction with Green FS 4079 for the basic disruptive camouflage on RAF aircraft. Initially only the upper surfaces were camouflaged, but during the mid-1970s (when the RAF toned down colours) this was used overall. This too is prone to fading in hot climates. US equivalent was used on the AV-8A.

3. Light Gull Grey FS 6440

Used on the undersides of RAF combat aircraft until the mid-1970s, it tended to show wear, oil and exhaust stains within a very short time. When the US began exporting the AV-8A to Spain the aircraft were finished in the standard USN/USMC colours of this shade on the upper surfaces and white undersides. It tended to wear with everyday use, and showed up dirt far more clearly.

4. Sea Grey FS 6118/ANA603

First used when the Sea Harrier FRS.1 entered service, and the standard Royal Navy upper colour from the end of World War 2. Also used by the USMC as the top colour camouflage on Harrier II aircraft. Did not tend to fade on the aircraft but was applied glossy to help fight salt corrosion. Aircraft finished in this did generally keep a good standard of appearance.

5. White FS 7875

This was used as the underside colour on Sea Harriers until 1982, when all were toned down for the Falklands War. Notorious for showing dirt and weathering almost straight away. White was also used as an underside colour on Spanish, Italian and Thai AV-8s.

6. RAF Ocean Grey FS 6270

Introduced as the alternative colour used on Sea Harriers along with Light Gull Grey under the wings. Tended to not wear as well as Gunship Light Grey FS 6118, and showed up dirt straight away. Also the finish 'flattened' much more, giving a very dirty look to the aircraft.

7. Dark Gull Grey ANA621/FS 6231

Used as the underside colour on USMC Harrier IIs. This colour tends to show dirt more – possibly due to the location of its use on the aircraft. Like most USN/USMC colours, when touched up there can be strong shade variations, which can give an aircraft a very worn appearance.

8. Dark Compass Grey FS 6320

Post the introduction of colour camouflage on USMC Harriers, this is the colour used for the fuselage sides as well as part of the upper surfaces. Like the upper colours it wears quite well on the uppers but not so well on the fuselage sides. Looks very grimy around the tail area where oil, exhaust and other dirt accumulate.